THE FUTURE OF
CHRISTIAN MARRIAGE

THE FUTURE OF CHRISTIAN MARRIAGE

Edited by
JOHN MARSHALL

Quentin de la Bedoyere
Jack Dominian
Gordon R. Dunstan
Rosemary Haughton

John Marshall
Patricia Marshall
Denis F. O'Callaghan
Bernard Parker

Douglas Woodhouse

GEOFFREY CHAPMAN
LONDON DUBLIN MELBOURNE 1970

Geoffrey Chapman Ltd
18 High Street, Wimbledon, London SW 19

Geoffrey Chapman (Ireland) Ltd
5-7 Main Street, Blackrock, County Dublin

265.5W
M356

81031318

© each chapter, 1969, the individual authors
© compilation, 1969, Geoffrey Chapman Ltd

First published 1969
Reprinted April 1970

ISBN 0 225.48862.0

Printed in Great Britain by Lowe & Brydone (Printers) Ltd., London

Contents

Introduction by John Marshall — 9

1. Christian marriage: the evolving situation — 11
   DENIS F. O'CALLAGHAN

2. The nature of marriage — 23
   JACK DOMINIAN

3. Education for marriage — 38
   QUENTIN DE LA BEDOYERE

4. Sex and Christian loving — 49
   JOHN MARSHALL

5. Married and other loves — 62
   PATRICIA MARSHALL

6. Christian marriage and Christian unity — 70
   GORDON R. DUNSTAN

7. Growth in marriage — 86
   ROSEMARY HAUGHTON

8. Birth regulation: future prospects — 96
   BERNARD PARKER

9. Marital problems: a strategy for service and research — 110
   DOUGLAS WOODHOUSE

Note on the contributors — 123

DEDICATED TO

MAURICE O'LEARY

on the occasion of the twenty-fifth anniversary
of his ordination to the priesthood

Introduction

THE Second Vatican Council marked the end of an era. The effects of the changes it wrought were felt not in Roman Catholic circles alone, but in the wider world beyond. Pope John opened a window on the world; the resulting draught was felt both outside and inside the Church.

In no sphere was the impact of the Council greater than in marriage. The immobilism which previously characterized the Church was nowhere more manifest than in its teaching on marriage. The fact that man is a historical being whose life, behaviour and relationships cannot be understood except in a historical context was little heeded in the theology of this important aspect of human life and experience. The deeper understanding provided by sacred and secular studies, biblical, theological, anthropological, sociological and psychological, was not allowed to disturb the tidy, juridical categories applied to the married state.

The Council initiated a change, not only by its own treatment of marriage, but by its attitude to the wider questions of revelation, the nature of the Church, religious freedom and so on. Immobilism was overcome and the Council set out as a pilgrim Church seeking the truth which is God.

Whilst there can be no doubt about the direction in which the Council went, there can be doubt about whether the pilgrimage continues in the right direction. Immobilists can still create obstacles in the path; innovators can still lead us into the wilderness. Continued effort is required, if progress towards truth is to be maintained, for just as a marriage is not made solely at the moment of the exchange of vows but must be worked at throughout life, so the Church cannot rest upon the achievement of the Council but must continue to study and pray in the decades that lie ahead.

This book is offered as a contribution, albeit small, towards this task. The contributors have endeavoured to look at marriage, not as it was or is, but as it seems to them it may become. In which direction is it going? Is this development healthy and to be encouraged? Does that development seem harmful and incompatible with Christian ideals? The book offers no blueprint. It is an exploration undertaken with a full sense of the responsibility that each of us has for the other.

A silver jubilee is also the end of an era, an era in a person's life. Whether it be twenty-five years of service in marriage or twenty-five years of service in the priesthood it is a time for looking forward as well as back, for making future plans as well as assessing past achievement. The fact that the greater part of Maurice O'Leary's twenty-five years as a priest has been devoted to the work of the Catholic Marriage Advisory Council makes it fitting that this book should be dedicated to him in celebration of this occasion. The search for truth which the Vatican Council initiated must proceed in a variety of ways. Truth in relation to marriage cannot be better sought than through the sympathetic, but objective, study of the experience of marriage of thousands of couples. Whether it is the difficulties with which they seek help when they come for counsel, or the hopes to which they aspire in their preparation for marriage, all can contribute to our knowledge and understanding. In dedicating the book to Maurice O'Leary we pay tribute to his achievement in this field, and pray that his work may continue and be blessed for years to come.

JOHN MARSHALL

May, 1969

1. Christian Marriage: The Evolving Situation

DENIS F. O'CALLAGHAN

No area of human life has so occupied the preacher, confessor and moralist as that of sex and marriage. 'Bishop condemns', 'Priest warns', 'Theologian forbids'—these phrases have echoed down the years and suggested to the man in the street that in the last analysis there is but one kind of morals, sexual morals, and that the moral value of marriage is that it takes the sin out of sex. The moralist and preacher, busily engaged in the task of spelling out a detailed code of sexual conduct, and so secure in the conviction that the answers were all there, rarely were called on to stop and ask the deeper questions, or wonder whether they had a satisfactory theology of marriage and sex at all. This is part of the price paid for being firmly rooted in a tradition. There is the danger that one will rest content with a closed, self-explanatory system, that firm assertion will be taken for reasoning, and that genuine questioning may be taken for disloyalty.

The real change in Catholic moral science today is a change of attitude in the matter of moral education. If moral doctrine is to affect men's lives today, it will have to face their questions and arouse their conviction. If one educates people to think independently and to take personal responsibility for what they think and do, one cannot insulate the field of morals from their consideration and responsibility. Indeed, it is in this field above all that personal consideration and responsibility should be active. The day of the *ipse dixit* is gone and the tendency to cling to it may discredit what is in effect a quite valid moral code. Moral living is something more than moral behaviour. Moral practice can be enforced by habit, convention, command or taboo, but in these cases one should speak of mores rather than of morals, of reflex action rather than of virtue. If moral conduct were nothing more than this, the human agent would really merit neither praise nor blame. Moral living or virtue is a matter of attitude rather than of habit, of understanding rather than of conditioning. If sex and morals are to be part of human and Christian life then man must appreciate their human and Christian meaning. To impose a code of morals without a process of moral education is to treat man as less than human and to deprive him of personal responsibility.

In our moral tradition there is a considerable element of reasoning, but sometimes it sounds suspiciously like a rationalization or justification of an already accepted position, as if the reasoning process were undertaken as a rather irksome and unnecessary chore before the moralist got down to the real task of setting out the principle in its concrete applications. Those who had reservations about the arguments or about accepted positions were easily disposed of as men of prejudice and questionable motive. But any attempt to moralize in closed circuit or to simplify problems out of existence is doomed to failure. The moral teacher who ignores or understates current questions about premarital sex, contraception, divorce or abortion loses his audience and effectively undermines their confidence in a code of morals which on its own merits may be substantially unassailable.

A realistic moral theology cannot ignore this attitude, nor can it ignore the findings of the positive sciences. Zoology, anthropology, empirical psychology and sociology have provided the moralist of the present time with a great deal of data on sexual behaviour, attraction and instinct, on the nature of human love and personal relationship, on the variety of marriage structures and sexual attitudes. These are facts of life and of nature as truly as the more familiar physiological ones. This is the language that a contemporary morality must speak if it is to get a hearing.

An adequate understanding of sex and sexual morals can come only from a proper understanding of marriage. Marriage institutionalizes sex, and it is only by studying it in that context that sex makes human and Christian sense. This statement of methodology seems obvious enough, but history shows that it needs emphasis. Sex tended to be studied as an activity of the individual rather than as a function of a unique relationship. It was judged unlawful for the single person, but marriage in some way rendered it lawful, and the intricacies of sexual casuistry suggested that even here it was principally a matter of the correct physical male-female interaction. Even if the moralist of previous generations had turned to marriage in his effort to understand sex, he would have found very little to go on. Marriage was very much a question of law, civil and canon, rather than of philosophy and theology. It is true that marriage is an important juridical fact and that family law is central in our social structures, deciding questions of domicile, parenthood, legitimacy and succession. Hence the web of legal terminology in which marriage and kinship are wrapped by civil lawyers. This legal bias is duplicated in canon law. The canonist sees marriage as a contract, a matter of rights and obligations. He is interested in the parties' freedom to contract a marriage, in the solemnities of the contract, in the permanence of the contractual bond, in the legal remedies for marital breakdown. Love, which decides the quality of the relationship, spirituality and Christian ideals are outside his professional ken because they cannot be codified.

In all this the lawyer is quite within his competence. What blame there is attaches to the theologian, who took over this legal systematization and accepted it as a satisfactory structure for a theology of marriage. The closed system of contract with its primary and secondary purposes gained self-sufficiency down through the generations. If a new insight was to win acceptance it had to find a niche in the system. If it did not bed in comfortably it was ignored as irrelevant or rejected as erroneous. Not only did the first tentative attempts at a theology of marriage in the decade 1930-40 founder here, but even Pius XI's encyclical *Casti Connubii* encountered the impasse. Whatever one's private assessment of *Casti Connubii* it was a serious attempt to view marriage in a wider theological perspective. It broke away from the contemporary legal formulation of contract and purposes and based its teaching on the Augustinian concept of the three blessings of marriage (children, partnership, permanence). It spoke of love as holding in Christian marriage 'what may be called a primacy of honour' : 'This mutual interior formation of husband and wife . . . may in a true sense be called the primary cause and reason of marriage . . . considered in its wider sense as a complete and intimate life-partnership and association.' (n. 23-24). This threatened to undermine the long accepted hierarchy of the ends or purposes of marriage—the primary end, the procreation and education of children; the secondary end, mutual help and a lawful outlet for passion. It is alleged that some translators of the encyclical left out the passage as needlessly confusing. Most authors tried to contain this concept of married love by forcing it in among the secondary purposes of marriage, and so the old system still creaked along.

Chiefly under the inspiration of Vatican II, the theology of marriage has broken new ground in recent years. It has at its disposal the unprecedented amount of data contributed by the positive sciences, it has made common cause with humanist and personalist philosophies in their search for meaning in life, and it has been inspired by the understanding which biblical theology has achieved of sex and marriage in the scriptures.

The points which came in for most theological comment at the Council were the central place given to love in marriage and the avoidance of the terms primary-secondary purposes. These terms were avoided because they suggested that partnership or the personal purpose of marriage was of less importance, and because they tended to perpetuate the fruitless controversy on the relative value of the two purposes. The attitude of the Council was that marriage had two essential purposes, parenthood and partnership, and that neither should be emphasized at the expense of the other. The Council also introduced an important change in methodology. In the Constitution on the Church in the Modern World marriage is treated primarily as institution rather than as contract. In fact, it avoids the term contract. In the few places where one would expect it, one finds instead *foedus matri-*

moniale, marriage covenant. This is far more than a question of language.

It is not to our purpose here to go into the reasons why the canon law of marriage centred on the contract. But it was well aware that marriage was a particular kind of contract. The partners were not free to decide what kind of relationship they would enter, since this was already determined or standardized. Therefore, canon law was conscious that there was an institution of marriage which qualified the consent. The Code of Canon Law referred to marriage as a perpetual and exclusive union, as an association with certain purposes and qualities.[1] *Casti Connubii* stated: 'The laws of marriage are independent of man's will and of any convention entered into by the partners' (n.5).

The fact that canon law began at two removes and was forced to import the institutional elements into the contract is evidence of incorrect method. The institution is primary in marriage. It determines that to which the partners give consent; the consent can be defined only in terms of the institution. Approached in this way consent will be seen as far more that the exchange of contractual rights to one another's body for the performance of sexual acts. It will be seen as the acceptance of a way of life together for the formation of a family unit in which new life is brought to maturity and in which husband and wife achieve fulfilment in life-long partnership.

In recent years lawyers have tended to swing towards emphasizing the institution. This tendency is directly motivated by the need to build firm barriers against divorce. To describe marriage as a contract suggests that the consent of the partners which made the marriage can also unmake it. To describe it in terms of institution indicates that it is something in its own right prior to any contract by the partners.

Whatever are the pros and cons in the legal field, there can be no doubt about the fact that the concept of institution provides a far more satisfactory approach for a theology of marriage. True, the term institution in current usage suggests a rather disembodied

[1] c. 1013, 1082, 1110.

legal system, but the technical meaning of the word is quite neutral and flexible. As applied to marriage and the family it presents them as established realities which have definite meaning in man's life, be it human or Christian.

Marriage in theology is a complex reality; it is an event both in the order of creation and in the order of redemption. The concept of institution must extend to take all this into account. As a human institution marriage is an exclusive and permanent community of love in which man and woman become husband and wife and father and mother with all that these terms imply. As a Christian institution marriage is a sacramental state established by Christ in which natural wedlock in all its elements is given a supernatural meaning or dimension and is directed towards the realization of the community of charity. It is from all this that matrimonial consent takes its meaning. It is the dedication of man and woman in partnership to a particular mission in the Church and the world, a mission which gives to marriage its own special meaning and spirituality. This force of the consent is best expressed by speaking of marriage vows rather than of contract.

Love is the heart of marriage. It gives to marriage its particularly human and personal note. It is the force which determines the quality of the partners' life together. Marriage may retain its legal stability, but if love is absent it is not the marriage that God's providence intended and that man's nature craves. In this context of love the purposes of marriage, parenthood and partnership are actualized. These joint purposes specify marriage and mark it off from other personal relationships. Both fall under the sway of love. Obviously, it is only in the atmosphere of love that new life finds a congenial home for its development and that the partners find an acceptable climate for their fulfilment. Love relates these two purposes so closely that they run parallel and intersect. Man and woman become supremely husband and wife when they become father and mother; the child comes to human maturity only in the company of a father and mother who are really husband and wife.

Thirty years ago Herbert Doms called for a clear distinction between the *meaning* of marriage and its *purposes*.[2] Marriage *is* in itself a reality of profound human significance before *being for* something else. This distinction would have saved the moralist of traditional bias from impoverishing the concept of love by relegating it among the secondary purposes of marriage. Doms appreciated that the love-community or, to use his own term, the two-in-oneness of the partners is not a purpose of marriage; it is a description of the marriage institution in itself. Here Vatican II bears him out. It describes the marriage institution as 'a community of love'. It states that 'by their very nature marriage itself and conjugal love are ordained for the procreation and education of children' (Constitution on the Church in the Modern World, n. 47-48).

Love is that mysterious force which draws two persons together precisely as persons so that their lives merge into one another. It is one of those primitive experiences of man which are difficult to define. Knowing and loving, those two primary activities which make man a person, are the hardest of all to explain. This does not make them any less real. For the lover there is nothing more real than falling in love, but his unique experience, because it is unique, does not admit of statement in cold rational terms; *le coeur a ses raisons*. . . . This is what makes poetry the language of love. It can break through the barriers of the commonplace and capture something of the indefinable. The effort to express and celebrate something of man's love for woman links the Song of Songs of the Bible with *The Extasie* of John Donne, the Troubadours of Provence with the modern pop-singers.

Identifying love as the core of marriage will raise problems for the moral theologian of legal cast. He will see it as an intangible which does not admit of strict definition or codification, as something which will queer a well-ordered system. True, it may be somewhat unmanageable and difficult to contain in legal terms, terms which are best suited to describing social realities and the externals of man's relationships, but if this is how things really are, it would be totally unscientific to deny reality in order to preserve spacious compactness in one's structures.

[2] *The Meaning of Marriage*, London, 1939.

Theology today must continue to present marriage as a structure in society with the responsibilities that this implies, but its most urgent task is to analyse the personal meaning of marriage. The growing awareness of the meaning and place of love in marriage is evident through a comparison between the rather ethereal treatment of married love (conjugal charity) in Pius XI's *Casti Connubii* and the more concrete description in Paul VI's *Humanae Vitae*. Theology has lagged here. Those engaged in pastoral work and in preparing people for marriage have been forced to improvise some working concept of married love as basis for their instruction. Real credit is due to these pioneering efforts. A great deal of positive research and critical analysis remains to be done before a balanced and satisfactory theology of love and marriage emerges. To appreciate these realities the moralist must assimilate the insights of biblical theology, he must listen to the experience of married people, he must learn from philosophy and literature which he may have once disregarded as humanist.

The general philosophy of friendship and interpersonal relationship is relevant to any description or analysis of married love, because it is a form of friendship. It differs from other forms of friendship in that it is sexual, and that in a very special way. Sexuality here is not only the male-female reality. It is that which commits man and woman to one another in all aspects of their joint natures, spiritual, intellectual, emotional and physical. In this way the masculine-feminine complement one another in what Doms called the two-in-oneness, that same two-in-oneness which the Greek myth of the Androgyne sought to explain. This two-in-oneness is characterized in two essential qualities of married love, exclusivity and permanence. Between married partners 'I love you' means 'I love you alone' and 'I love you always'. The suggestion that some third party shares or may share this love or that it is not permanent in intent destroys it at source. On this understanding divorce and infidelity should be regarded as failures in love, and an incapacity to make a permanent exclusive commitment in love should be regarded as a personality fault.

Married love is sexual in a particular way in that it has as its particular expression the act of sexual intercourse. The act of love signifies the self-gift of the partners to one another, and seals the oneness of mind and heart which their common life and love requires. Sex as procreative and sex as expressive of married love are in no sense in opposition. The controversies which have grown up around the purposes of marriage and around contraception may have suggested some such opposition by playing off one aspect against the other. But these aspects intertwine and explain one another. Since the love of husband and wife leads to the child, the child is not in any sense an intruder in their love. He is conceived in their love and in him their love lives. This procreative quality of married love simply reaffirms the creativity which is found in all genuine love.

Love humanizes both sex and procreation. The fact that sex is the expression of love puts the concept of the marriage due in its proper perspective. It is not a matter of one partner claiming contractual rights to the body of the other on a title of strict justice. It is not a matter of one partner demanding satisfaction of his physical needs, and treating the other as an object of sensual pleasure. It is a question of signifying their love for one another in mutual thoughtfulness and consideration. This human appreciation of sex corrects the exaggerated interpretation which a more legal tradition imposed on the Pauline directive of rendering the marriage due. It was Sanchez, in his classical manual *De Matrimonio*, who stated that the marriage due could be extorted by violence where persuasion failed, and that the right was so unquestionable that there was no need to appeal to the courts of justice to gain possession.[3] The saner moral tradition and concrete pastoral practice offset this doctrine of legalized rape by outlining a great number of 'excusing causes'. The recent encyclical of Pope Paul puts the matter much more positively:

> Men rightly observe that to force the use of marriage on one's partner without regard to his or her condition or personal and reasonable wishes in the matter, is no true act of love, and therefore offends the moral order in its particular application to the intimate relationship of husband and wife.

[3] Lib. 2, disp. 22, n. 13.

If there is one lesson which the moralist should learn from a thousand years of casuistry it is that the details of the marriage bed are best left to the married couple.

Against the background of married love the meaning of parenthood also comes out in clearer perspective. The refusal to serve new life through the selfish exclusion of children is a distortion of the partners' love and closes them in on themselves. The search for sensual enjoyment without responsibility erodes love and eliminates that creativity which is its dynamism. In effect, their love is a particular kind of love, love in the context of marriage, love which aims to form a family unit. The love of husband and wife is thus complemented in the love of parent and child. Therefore, the family unit embraces a double kind of love, a love of free selection by which man and woman sought one another out and through which they come to unite their lives, and a love of natural acceptance, by which the partners accept as their very own the fruit of their love and of their united lives. Both these patterns of love indicate relationships between persons. They differ in that the first attaches to this unique person and so is radically unexplainable, whereas the second attaches to the child as a common product and possession, and nature itself gives reasons for this.

The love which is open to life is concerned not just with bringing new life into being. Its concern extends to the forming of the human person, to the spiritual, social, emotional, material conditions in which new life grows to maturity. Hence the parenthood which love requires is responsible parenthood. Love is realistic. Generous it must be, but it must also be provident. It cannot close its eyes to the factors which determine the pattern of its generosity.

In the above pages we have been dealing with marriage as a human institution, as an event in the order of creation. Marriage is also a Christian institution, a sacrament, an event in the order of redemption. It is unique among the sacraments in that it has no specific ritual or sacramental sign. The sign of the sacrament is the exchange of marriage vows, by which husband and wife, the ministers of the sacrament, commit themselves to marriage in the Lord, to a way of life which is directed towards the realization of Christ's kingdom, the extension of the community of charity. Marriage is also exceptional in that it is not a transient sacramental act but a permanent sacramental state. Cardinal Bellarmine's words are often quoted here:

> The sacrament of matrimony may be considered in two ways: in the moment of its accomplishment and in its permanency afterwards. This sacrament, in fact, is similar to the eucharist, which likewise is a sacrament not only in the moment of its accomplishment but in its permanency afterwards. For as long as husband and wife live, their fellowship is always the sacrament of Christ and the Church (n. 116).

The marriage vow is a dedication to a mission in the Church; it consecrates the relationship of husband and wife and constitutes it a permanent warranty of Christ's presence, sanctifying the family and, through the family, the world.

On this understanding the sacrament or the supernatural in Christian marriage is explained as a deepening or new dimension in the significance of natural wedlock. Every aspect of marriage in the order of creation is given new force or meaning in the order of redemption.

Marriage consent is not just the acceptance of another human person as a partner for life; it is the acceptance of another Christian as a partner for eternity. It is not just the acceptance of wedlock as giving a secular mission in the world to give and form new life, to achieve human fulfilment, to subdue the earth and to advance culture. It is also the acceptance of an ecclesial mission in the Church to give and form faith, to sanctify the family and, through the family, the world of men.

Love in the Christian family has the supernatural force of charity. It is the mediation and reflection of that love which unites the persons in the Trinity. It is God's gift of himself to man. 'God is love; he who abides in love abides in God and God abides in him' (1 Jn 4: 16). This charity permeates both the love of husband and wife and the love of parent and child. The partners are called on to love one another as Christ loved the Church (Eph. 5 : 25). Their love must be as wholehearted as the love of Christ, who gave his life for his loved one, it must be as permanent as the love of him who promised to be with his Church for all time. Their mutual love is the climate in which each works out the salvation of the other: 'The unbelieving husband is consecrated through his wife, and the unbelieving wife is consecrated through her husband' (1 Cor. 7 : 14). The parents are called on to love their children as Christ's little ones, entrusted to them to bring to him. The Roman Ritual reminds parents: 'It will be your duty and privilege to bring them up as good citizens of this world and worthy members of the mystical body of Christ, so that they may one day inherit his kingdom in heaven.'

A great deal remains to be done in clarifying the various aspects which constitute the institution of marriage, human and Christian. Both dimensions require development, but in a very real sense the analysis of the human reality is the prior necessity. Until this structure is satisfactorily described, theological concepts will be crude and generalized. The terms which express Christian marriage emanate from the human structure and a theology which ignores this will wander into unreality. In an institution which so combines human and Christian life, God the Creator and God the Redeemer speak very much the same language.

2. *The Nature of Marriage*
JACK DOMINIAN

IF the average educated Catholic was asked to give a short account of the teaching of his Church on marriage he would be able to offer some or all of the following points. He would know that if possible he should marry a fellow Catholic in a Catholic Church; a registry office marriage would be wrong. He should not give in to impurity before marriage and, after it, should not use contraceptives. Marriage is for children and therefore the use of sex is intimately connected with them. A large family is a good thing and the children should be preferably sent to a Catholic school. Divorce is forbidden and so is infidelity. Marriage is a sacrament, but with further pressure on this point little else would emerge. Marriage is for love, but once again there would be difficulties about further development of this point.

All this would be available in the standard manuals, presented in a less fragmented form than above but until very recently unlikely to contain any further detailed development. Marriage, like other aspects of life, was understood through the law, a matter of taking the right course at the right time and place. Theology, such as it was, concentrated on the legal aspects and the conditions under which a valid marriage was contracted. This has been, and continues to be, of the greatest importance because once a marriage between two baptized persons is declared to be valid and consummated, as far as the Church is concerned, the conditions are fulfilled for life-long indissolubility.

According to present legislation, the validity of marriage can be challenged under three categories only. The first is concerned with the capacity to make the contract. According to present legislation, there are twelve diriment impediments which relate to age, abduction, crime, spiritual relationship, impotence, sacred orders, marriage bond, vow of chastity, consanguinity, affinity, public decorum and disparity of cult. Apart from impotence, the other grounds contribute little to nullity. Secondly, there are irregularities of juridical form, which are undoubtedly used as an excuse for some other difficulty and bring the charges against the Church that they constitute a back-door entry to divorce. Thirdly, each of the parties must will, that is to say give his consent freely; must will to marry, which means to give assent to the essential characteristics of Christian marriage (permanency, procreation, fidelity), and must will to marry a specific person.

Thus, when a question of nullity is entertained by an ecclesiastical court all these issues are solemnly examined by an exhaustive series of questions which, valid as they are, have little relevance to the reality of Christian marriage as experienced by the partners. Christian marriage, seen in these legalistic terms and communicated as such for hundreds of years inside Christendom, has reduced God's precious gift to man to an incomprehensible pittance which has become for outside observers an interesting anachronism, a fascinating curio, little understood but conveniently attacked when the occasion arises.

From the depths of such doldrums Vatican II produced some, but not enough, revitalizing principles. The obsolete, confusing language of primary and secondary ends has been discarded. A new emphasis on love is to be found in the opening paragraph of the document which describes matrimony as a 'community of love'. But despite this considerable advance, in one way or another the document reiterates the limited formulations of the past. Thus the marriage bond is the essence of marriage.

> It is rooted in the conjugal covenant of irrevocable personal consent. Hence, by that human act whereby spouses mutually bestow and accept each other, a relationship arises which by divine will and in the eyes of society too is a lasting one.

This traditional emphasis on a particular moment of time at the onset of marriage fits poorly with the notion of a life-long union and has rightly drawn criticism, albeit somewhat exaggerated, from Karl Barth, of the Church's view of matrimony as nothing but a doctrine of the wedding ceremony.

Although the previous terminology has been dropped, the so-called five essential ends, procreation and education of children, mutual help, sexual fulfilment and conjugal love, reappear in different language. Thus 'Marriage and conjugal love are by their nature ordained toward the begetting and educating of children'. This statement is in fact only partially true because it does not take into serious consideration the years of marriage prior to procreation and the many years (running into one, two or three decades) when the children have grown up, nor has there ever been an adequate understanding of sterile unions.

Mutual help is mentioned but not in any way elaborated.

> Thus a man and a woman . . . render mutual help and service to each other through an intimate union of their persons and of their actions. Through this union they experience the meaning of their oneness and attain to it with growing perfection day by day.

The wording cannot be faulted but it has to be admitted it says very little about the nature of the mutual help.

Sexual fulfilment is dismissed briefly but with dignity.

> The actions within marriage by which the couple are united intimately and chastely are noble and worthy ones. Expressed in a manner which is truly human, these actions signify and promote that mutual self-giving by which spouses enrich each other with a joyful and thankful will.

This is virtually all that is said about sexuality within marriage except for the usual warnings about its misuse.

Conjugal love receives special attention in the document. It is described as 'eminently human'. It involves the 'good of the whole person'. It pervades 'the whole of their lives'. It is capable of 'healing', 'perfecting', and 'exalting gifts of grace and of charity'. The penultimate paragraph on conjugal love asks for a cultural, psychological and social renewal on behalf of marriage and the family.

One cannot but concur with this plea but I believe that here as elsewhere it is necessary first for the Church to re-examine its own sources of truth and the presentation of the latter, before Christianity can impinge meaningfully on the world. In this context I believe that the current presentation of the meaning of marriage is basically a fragmentation of the truth, making little impact because it does not reflect accurately either marriage or the essentials of Christian marriage. This is not to say that all the relevant signposts mentioned have no intrinsic validity. They have, but they fail to do justice to marriage because they spring from traditions which aimed to justify the use of sexuality within marriage and had limited and inadequate understanding of the psychology of men and women. Thus while I wholeheartedly welcome the emphasis on love, I regret the absence in the document of Vatican II and in the encyclical *Humanae Vitae* of a return to the biblical notion of marriage as a relationship. Hereafter in this paper I shall examine marriage as a relationship or more correctly a series of relationships.

Christian marriage is a God-given, life-long community, created to ensure the most appropriate conditions for the promotion of life, the life of the children and that of the spouses. It is based on a series of relationships of love which, in a chronological order, are those of the spouses, the spouses and the children and the children among themselves. It is upon the physical, psychological and social integrity of these relationships, participating in the sacramental life of grace, that the essence of marriage ultimately rests.

Increasingly our understanding of marriage suggests that it is not primarily *for* something, it *is* something, a series of relationships which allow certain events to take place within it, which intrinsically belong to the state.

I believe that each aspect of the relationship should possess minimum degrees of fulfilment which will evolve continuously, setting new standards in each successive age, reflecting deeper and wider understanding of the appropriate standards of human dignity for each epoch. Thus these minimum requirements will not be static and their absence will invalidate the concept of marriage. Furthermore, since the presence or absence of these human characteristics will become evident only in the course of marriage, the significance of the initial ceremony has to be examined afresh. It is my contention that while marriage truly begins at this initial moment of commitment, it is not actually realized until the second phase when the manifested relationship confirms or denies the promises rendered at that initial moment. Such a conceptual development of marriage would incorporate the present view which accepts that marriage is made by the exchange of consent but would extend the Church's ability to declare certain marriages as null and void at a later stage if the minimum requirements are not fulfilled.

Thus if Christian marriage is to be considered a life-long union, as the scriptures insist is the appropriate model for man, then clearly men and women must carry within themselves the minimum human characteristics, realized, or in potential, which will meet each other's needs *throughout the duration of marriage*. The life-long views taken at the commencement of the union commit each partner to fulfil the minimum requirements of the relationship over a number of years, meeting personal and interpersonal needs which evolve and alter.

Insistence on the presence of minimum requirements is an aspect of marriage largely dictated by my conviction that the Church condemns innumerable people to a so-called marriage which never existed because the spouses promised to each other aspects of themselves which they willed consciously to give but which were unavailable in reality, or, if initially available, were not able to be sustained later on, and this is incompatible with a life-long relationship. At this point I am well aware of the criticisms that will be directed to such an approach to marriage. It will be said that people are not always capable of maintaining the initial promises, and any diminution of strict observance of the contract will lead to widespread damage to the stability of marriage. This is a view of some, but limited, validity. The immediate answer to this objection is that while the partners will assess their incompatibility the final judgment will be based on the exacting requirements of Christian marriage by a competent authority appointed by and in the name of the whole people of God. Such an authority should in the future contain suitable lay people as well as clerics.

Nevertheless, I do not believe that people will resort to such relief as a wholesale escape from responsibility in the hope of easier fulfilment and gratification. All Christian life implies suffering and sacrifice and this belongs as much to marriage as to all other aspects of life. But such suffering must be creative and purposeful if it is to have validity. For the overwhelming majority of people marriage is the single most vital experience in their lives, in which they invest their highest aspirations for happiness. Few give up these hopes without a persistent and dogged fight, for they have little to gain and much to lose by admitting personal failure of such magnitude.

So far I have been concerned with the notion of minimum requirements and with the view that these characteristics should exist in the partners, rendering them capable of initiating and sustaining a viable relationship throughout marriage in a mutually matching manner for successive phases of the marriage cycle. The emphasis so far has been on absolute minimums without which viable relationships cannot exist. Beyond this there is the limitless goals of *mutual growth*, so that each aspect of marriage should be considered in terms of its initiation, development and decline. Thus a mutual decline in sexual functioning belongs to some of the later stages and gradual diminution of physical, psychological and social functioning will belong to marriage in its later stages as vigorous development belongs in its earlier period. The concept of relationship, however, underlies the need to examine marriage always in terms of mutual needs. With these principles in mind the physical and psychological relationships can now be examined in some detail.

It is within marriage and marriage alone that a full sexual relationship is considered appropriate in Christianity. What is a full sexual relationship? Sexuality has been bedevilled by a tradition which has been obsessionally preoccupied with instinctual gratification. So long as sex is seen purely in instinctual terms then clearly the behaviour appropriate to it must safeguard man from becoming a prey to excessive, uncontrolled sexual pleasure. There is little doubt in my mind that the tradition which emphasized exclusively the connection between sex and procreation was not merely reflecting the biologically obvious but was a clear-cut attempt to contain and defuse something dangerous.

It is only in relatively recent times, in the course of the last few decades, that there has been a widespread awakening to the reality that everything rendered available by God in the creation of man must have the potentiality of excellence if properly used. The full use of sex extends well beyond a view of marital chastity in terms of quantity and biological appropriateness. It reaches well beyond the openness of each act to life. Human sexuality within marriage is the expression of a delicate balance of the biological, psychological and social. It finds its completion in the quality of these three characteristics blending together and realized to their maximum potential as often as possible.

Biologically there must exist a physiological and anatomical intactness which will permit normal libido, sexual arousal and the completion of the sexual act. Impotence, which prevents consummation, has been recognized by the Church as a ground for dissolubility but the time is now ripe for an extension of this principle. Thus marriages in which one or more sexual acts have been completed but in which sexual activity ceases soon afterwards, stand at the present moment as valid marriages. Such a view is quite incompatible with the nature of marriage in which the sexual act is the central and recurring act by which the specific quality of the relationship is enacted. Sexual intercourse must be considered a right belonging to both partners, throughout marriage, even though not exercised. If this right is conceded, then naturally the question of frequency will arise. How often should this act be demanded as a right? Clearly this must be judged according to the appropriate physical and psychological norms for successive phases of the marital cycle.

Biological integrity is not exhausted by the penetration of the penis into the vagina and the subsequent deposition of semen. Genital union is but one part of a total physical involvement and sexual union involves the offering of every part of the body to the partner in a way that enhances physical awareness, excitation and fulfilment. This is an infinitely more exacting task than mere genital penetration for through this exchange each partner is prompted to a deepening awareness of their own body. Now perhaps for the first time they experience regions of themselves which hitherto were blind spots merely to be washed and covered with clothing. These are gradually transformed into exquisite sources of physical gratification extending the sexual identity of the person. The delicate caressing and awakening of the body as part of the preparation prior to sexual consummation belongs undoubtedly to the quality of sexual exchange which transcends mere genital union.

Currently such bodily involvement is of particular importance for the woman, whose equal involvement in the exchange demands that she is treated by her husband with much greater care. Her body is much more than a receptacle for her husband's semen. The deposition of semen and the fertilization of ova are not in themselves too exacting procedures but the ingenuity and skill in mutual awakening and extension of the body as a sexual object requires infinite patience, care and gentility in a process of mutual emotional awakening. The quality of this exchange in each and every act is infinitely more important than the biological opportunity for fertilization. For each act carries the recurrent potential of recognizable acceptance, reassurance and comforting of each other as the most vital person in their life.

Sexual integrity thus means the realization of the physical and emotional potential of the partners in a harmonious and complementary way. Implicit in this assumption is an education at home and school which allows the growing person access to knowledge and a positive approach to sexuality from the earliest years of life. Given such an affirmative background, and in the absence of any anatomical or physiological malfunctioning, the quality of the sexual experience ultimately depends on the overall emotional relationship of the couple. There cannot be sexual harmony unless the emotional needs of the couple on a wider front are met and the nature of these needs will depend both on a deepening awareness of the psychology of interpersonal relationship and a heightening social awareness that this aspect of marriage is of vital importance. So long as marriage concentrated on achieving ends without paying due attention to the quality of the various relationships, insufficient care was given to the personal feelings and emotions of the couple. As these aspects receive increasing attention and as the woman shares in the standards that are acceptable to her as a wife, there is inevitably a need to re-examine the emotional qualities needed.

The study of marriage is still in too early a stage to select with confidence the major psychological traits without which a developing marital relationship cannot be achieved. What follows are some characteristics which, while in no way comprehensive, do play an important part in the relationship.

The first, and probably one of the commonest problems that is encountered by a couple, is the absence in one or both of a minimum emotional independence to sustain separation from the parental home without excessive anxiety. However much the person desires to marry, leave home and set up on their own, they may be overwhelmed at the thought of having to survive without parental support.

The union of one or two such people may be punctuated by difficulties in the engagement period when the mounting anxiety over the prospective break from home or the challenge of the new demands may prove overwhelming, leading to psychological breakdown, a suicidal attempt or the breaking off of the engagement. Alternatively such people drift on with an apparently endless engagement and the marriage is delayed for a variety of reasons.

If and when such a marriage takes place and the couple live near one or both parental homes, the outcome may prove disastrous early on. The complaints are standard. Both will accuse each other of spending more time in their parental than marital home, caring too little for each other and being over-influenced by the parents. This is all perfectly true and, if the parents find the separation even more painful than their child, they will aid and abet the marital breakdown by reinforcing their offspring's criticism of the partner, gradually paralysing any hope of reconciliation. If they retire into the background, discourage the use of their home, but give support at a distance, there is a chance for the successful negotiation of this early phase.

Another common emotional difficulty does not arise early but much later on. Here I am referring to the union of a dependent spouse, characterized by a high degree of anxiety, the need for reassurance and for the presence of a more independent, strong and often apparently dominant person to complement their needs and thus to act as a continuation of the parental support. All goes well for a number of years but gradually the dependent partner begins to outgrow their initial fears or, with a growth of confidence, wants to establish new roles in the relationship. If the wife is such a person, she may now want to select more freely her own clothes, the places she wishes to visit, the people she wants to meet and befriend, to have a voice in how money is going to be spent, etc., etc. Similarly the husband may wish to have greater freedom with the money he earns, experiment without previous approval with regard to work, friends and leisure spent outside the home, and to have a greater say in the decisions within the home and in the upbringing of the children.

Many couples who marry on such a discrepant emotional level gradually adapt to the partner's emergence. Trouble is confined to those situations when the dominant partner will neither yield nor adapt to the new needs of their spouse. Increasingly he or she will be experienced as an oppressor and a jailer with endless arguments, quarrels, sexual alienation and possibly physical violence. This situation will be tolerated for a period of time until someone next door, in the town or village, at the office or the factory, begins to respond to the obvious sadness and misery of the individual. Such affairs carry all the dangers that similarly afflicted individuals, with an above average propensity to emotional difficulties, will gravitate towards one another, storing up more trouble for each other. On the other hand, the befriending person may offer for the first time an appropriate response to the man or woman who now feels truly appreciated in a manner befitting their newly discovered self. In this way people speak of falling *out* of love with one person and *in* love with another. Outsiders may comment that such behaviour is irresponsible; in fact it represents a true development in the nature of the personality which requires, but could not receive, a matching response.

Such a situation would naturally not exist if the marriage is considered only in its externals of erecting a home, providing the material needs of sustenance and procreating children. All this can be achieved by two people who become total strangers to one another as a result of differential growth, unrecognized and unappreciated by the other.

Another feature with which psychiatry is very familiar is the presence of one or two people loaded with a sense of their own inadequacy, badness and incompetence, who reject themselves totally and who consider their presence as highly damaging to others. Such people have often grown up in homes where they failed totally to receive the experience of their own acceptability in terms of being wanted, appreciated or loved for their own sake. In such an environment the opposite trend occurred, namely a strong sense of their inability to believe that there existed anything in their make-up which was worthy of love. Such a person has a very high need to be loved but a very low capacity to accept it. Loving approaches will be constantly misinterpreted. Such a situation will have a direct and destructive impact on sexual relationships. Both partners, if they share the trait, will be constantly on tenterhooks as to whether they are really wanted by the other and will rely heavily on signs of encouragement and reassurance that will overcome their hesitation. Since their inner world will forbid such overtures of attention, they will find it difficult to ease progress towards each other. When the wife alone suffers from such a state, sexual approaches to her will be particularly trying. If the husband is not able to show unequivocally his interest in her as a person with love-making prior to intercourse, she will experience the act as nothing less than a crude violation of her body. If he does show all the care she deserves, she will find it very difficult to fit such attention within a framework of her own feelings of inferiority. Such a response will deter any but the most confident of husbands. If the husband ceases sexual activity, this will confirm the wife's fears about herself and a vicious circle is established. Indeed it requires emotional maturity and persistence of the highest order to overcome the emotional reluctance of another person to be loved. In the presence of two such affected personalities the chances of effecting a relationship of love are obviously very limited indeed. Unfortunately when such a marriage breaks up there is less of a chance for the next one to succeed since the person carries over within himself or herself the same characteristics.

Jealousy and envy are two words widely used in describing marital disharmony situations. Jealousy indicates the presence of hostility towards another person who threatens to compete successfully for the attention of the spouse. Jealousy is often accompanied by complaints of insufficient attention received. Envy is a feeling directed towards another person, in the case of marriage the spouse, whose success and attributes are resented with underlying feelings of destroying or taking away whatever is possessed.

Insufficient attention, jealousy and envy are traits which develop in people who have been grossly deprived of due attention in the course of their childhood development. Such situations often carry family backgrounds in which the child did not experience a sufficiency of trust or an abundance of availability of the right quality. It experienced too much and too often the dread of loss, abandonment and the quality of unreliable and unpredictable behaviour. The consequences of such an upbringing are a deep fear of loss, and jealousy is a behaviour pattern which reacts angrily at the slightest possibility of any loss of attention, while living constantly on the threshold of the panic of being abandoned.

Envy develops in similar circumstances with the addition that the parent presents an image of strength, grandeur, confidence, wisdom and excellence, which is unavailable to the child who feels inadequate by comparison. Side by side with a sense of respect and admiration for such a parent, there is entertained, often unconsciously, an immense hatred and desire to destroy, to take away from them or to humiliate them. If the spouse is married on a basis of such an admiring similarity, then these feelings of envy will be expressed destructively in the marriage.

The results of such a deprived childhood lead to the development of over-demanding, attention-seeking, jealous and envious men and women. Their needs are so marked that in marriage there is likely to be exploitation. The partner exists only to the degree that he or she is available to meet the missing needs. The partner is less a husband or a wife but rather the hated and defective parent who owes restitution. This leads to patterns of conduct marked by the term selfishness, self-centredness, narcissism etc.

When two such intensely deprived people marry then the relationship may come to an early end as their mutual exploitation overwhelms them. Another possibility, however, is the establishment of a triangular or quartet situation in which the marriage continues but extramarital affairs of a temporary or semi-permanent nature continue to answer the missing or excessive needs of each partner. With the passage of time there is enough growth to diminish the requirements with a gradual stabilization of the union. Otherwise these unions are extremely unstable, with the partners drifting from one unsatisfactory affair or marriage to another.

Yet another pattern is the presence of one such deprived person and a partner of a more stable disposition who endures many years of little attention, much infidelity and many hurts. They may stay on for the sake of the children until they have grown up but suddenly their patience becomes exhausted and they will quit their partner for another one who may be able to offer them love for the first time.

All these patterns are examples of a theory of marital pathology which is gaining ground both here and in the United States. This theory, called object-relations theory, takes the view that the growing person needs a certain minimum facilitation to achieve a normal personality. The presence or absence of such facilities will be provided in childhood from birth onwards by the parents with whom the vital bonds of intimate relationship will be formed. If these bonds are defective, they are likely to be repeated in the only other intimate relationship, namely marriage. Marriage seen in this light requires an emotional development of sufficient degree in which all the principal phases of childhood are adequately negotiated and the young man or woman can experience herself and her partner free from the residues of undeveloped or maldeveloped childhood traits.

The document on marriage of Vatican II refers to love as being capable of healing and perfecting. These words describe accurately the therapeutic effect of the spouses on each other as they fulfil, each in a different way, the emotional needs which will allow the partner to experience trust, acceptance and appreciation perhaps for the first time in their life. When this healing removes the depths of deprivation, there is an ever open opportunity to go beyond the bare necessities and, like sexuality, to develop further awareness of the potential in each other, perfecting their respective emotional competence.

In addition to such a theory, there are also certain patterns of behaviour, frequently seen in marriage, which are highly damaging to a close relationship. I refer to those men and women who have a very low capacity to tolerate frustration, in the presence of which they react violently and excessively; or those who have an equally low threshold to frustration but react to it by long periods of withdrawal in which anger is expressed by a refusal to forgive or forget. The quick temper which is over in minutes is nothing like as damaging as the presence of either persistent withdrawal or expressed hostility. When such patterns of reaction are associated with prominent features of dependence, self-esteem or deprivation difficulties, then we are often at the very heart of a situation in which marriage borders on the impossible.

These examples are but a few of the complicated psychological patterns encountered in marriage. Their recognition and the attention they are receiving is a reflection of an increasing awareness of marriage as a relationship of the partners prior to and long after the procreation and education of children. Indeed marriage as a relationship of the partners must be examined separately from the concept of the family characterized by the presence of the children.

Such a view of marriage will render meaningful for the first time sterile marriages which in Catholic theology have always been treated as the poor cousins of fertile unions, will focus attention on marriage as a continuing entity after the children have grown up, leaving a period sometimes of several decades and will, I trust, emphasize above all that no child should be conceived until the spouses have a stable enough relationship to give their offspring the attention, care and love they have a right to receive. The presence of children establishes a host of new relationships between parents and children and among the children themselves which deserves detailed examination, but now we are entering strictly the world of the family.

Such a re-orientation of marriage in terms of on-going and continuous relationships, requiring characteristics in the partners to meet and match changing needs in the marriage cycle, will have widespead repercussions for the Catholic theology of the future. But marriage seen primarily as a relationship and not as a legal contract will be a direct return to the utterances of both the Old and the New Testament, in which marriage is seen and described in terms of a relation between God and the people in the Old Testament, and between Christ and his Church in the New.

Such an approach is perfectly consistent with all our advances in understanding the real meaning of marriage in an age of increasing equality between the sexes, another feature heralded by St Paul and awaiting fulfilment in our age. Indeed such an orientation offers no threat to Christian marriage and brings it much closer to the pattern which, in his eternal wisdom, the Creator instituted for man.

3. *Education for Marriage*
QUENTIN DE LA BEDOYERE

JOSEPHINE is a friend of ours. On her last visit we knew from the tense expression on her face that she had a problem—and, at eighteen, problems and boy friends often go together. This weekend her parents were away and her current young man was making the most of the situation. Josephine has only known him for a few weeks but, rather to her surprise, the relationship has quickly become somewhat intense. 'Even if he only touches my shoulder, I quiver', was how she put it. He had called the previous evening and they had spent most of the time in bed together. Josephine is a sensible girl and, being without contraceptives, intercourse itself had not taken place. But, she told us, the coming evening made the crossing of this rubicon inevitable and, congested as she is by desire, the relief which she believes intercourse will give her is a pressing, almost suffocating, need. With a great effort of will—Josephine is a shy, self-conscious girl —she obtained contraceptives, but, suddenly feeling trapped by the situation, she has come to talk it out with friends she feels she can trust.

Poor Josephine! Her predicament is not unusual. Of course, she brings to it her own particular heredity and background, an outlook formed by her personal history and previous experiences of relationship, but she has, in common with her generation, an orientation towards sexual morality not altogether comprehensible to her elders, who took the bombing of Dresden in their stride. While the techniques of social measurement are too young to allow an effective comparison of the actual behaviour of successive generations, a fundamental change in attitude has certainly occurred. Except for peripheral issues, such as the exploitation of others, sexual behaviour outside marriage is no longer a moral question. But if, like us, she takes her values largely from the climate of her generation, her confidence sometimes masks an uncertainty, a dis-ease which she is anxious to hide. Josephine, in fact, is far from sure how she ought to handle the situation. The questions for her are seen as concerned with practical consequences or personal integrity—and if she is not aware of how these relate to the very moral categories she has abandoned, that is scarcely her fault.

Although the figures which would enable us to chart the changes in behaviour are lacking, the current situation is very clear. In the early part of the sixties, it was established that about half the teenage population would be involved in fairly serious sex play by the time they reached their twenties, and about half of that number again would have experienced sexual intercourse. Catholic young people do not differ substantially from their peers, although the number of Catholic girls recorded as having experienced sexual intercourse was somewhat lower than the average.[1] A much more restricted survey taken recently and compared with earlier figures would suggest that the proportion of teenagers involved has grown considerably since that time, which will scarcely surprise anyone who has had the confidence of young people over the period.[2] Presumably this trend will have a saturation point, but I think it is optimistic to suppose that it will reverse substantially—on some kind of pendulum theory. The pendulum has been given a very definite bias; first, by the ability to separate intercourse from its natural consequences and second, by the development of our understanding of the expression of relationship through its means.

These facts are of central importance in any consideration of education for marriage; indeed they are part of it. Part of it because what a person is, in his attitudes and thoughts, is in large measure his historical self—what his previous experiences have made him. Whether our young people are educated for marriage

[1] Schofield, *The Sexual Behaviour of Young People*, Longmans, London, 1965 (also Pelican, 1968).
[2] Dr William Kind, survey of 18 year olds, compared with a similar investigation in 1963, *The Observer*, 9 Feb. 1969.

is not in question, only whether the process is for good or for ill. The thread which runs through the pattern of development is the experience of love. We are told that this is critical in early childhood where the basic orientation towards other people is shaped through the initial encounters of infancy. Adolescence is a similarly formative process in which the new factor of conscious sexuality must be successfully grafted into love, if the whole person is to be formed. No one need approve of the moral standpoint of young people—after all, they do not approve of ours—but it is necessary to accept that it exists and to take its implication : at the present time, and perhaps increasingly in the future, intense sexual experiences are being incorporated by a majority of young people into their education for marriage. The useful question is to ask how we can help them to benefit from the positive elements in their experience and enable them to grow through it towards maturity—just as we help young children to profit from the experiences, bad and good, of infancy.

But an adolescent is not a young child. The six year old may pick up a few bumps and bruises as it experiments its way through childhood, but the equivalent fumblings of a fifteen year old may pick up personal tragedy, disease or a baby. One would have to be wilfully blind to think that a liberal attitude towards sexual morality is currently leading us into a golden age of human fulfilment and personal happiness. And those who, like me, approach this question from a Catholic Christian standpoint would seem to be committed to a view of sexual intercourse which would regard marriage as its only proper environment and, by the same token, would disapprove of the intimacies which in their innate tendencies are inextricably linked to the full expression of sexual love.

However compelling these arguments may be, Josephine does not think very much of them. It is possible that the practical dangers may influence her behaviour, but it is more likely that they will seem as remote to her as the danger in crossing the road. In fact Josephine intends to avoid the obvious results by her visit to the chemist and, in doing so, demonstrates an uncharacteristic prudence. Her friends, who rationalize their activities by an appeal to the safety of contraceptives, have a very cavalier attitude to their employment in practice. Nor would she be influenced by an appeal to authority, whether of her parents or of her religion. Why should she be? She is at a transitional stage where the acceptance of authority that is proper and reasonable for a child has been largely abandoned in preparation for adulthood. Later if she is helped—or at least not hindered—in her progress to maturity, she will once more perceive the value of authority when she re-discovers it in an adult context. At this particular point everything is in the melting pot, which is just as it should be.

Everyone knows what the word adolescent means: the process of growing from a child into an adult. Yet few people take its meaning seriously. There are those who treat adolescents like children and that is dangerous; others treat them like adults and that is disastrous. Josephine merely wants to be treated as she is, a person in the process of ceasing to be what she once was and not yet arrived at what she is to become. She may not put this in so many words, sharing with her contemporaries the view that the process is completed by the ability to produce a Zapata moustache or fill a Little X bra; but that is an understandable exercise in wishful thinking. In reality, to treat her other than she really is shows a lack of that essential respect without which effective help is impossible.

The attitude towards authority which I have already mentioned provides a good example of this respect in action. If Josephine is at a stage when a sceptical scrutiny of authority is a necessary element in growth towards an adult grasp in this area, it will scarcely be helpful to chide her, either for her defiance or her immaturity. A proper respect for her adolescence would rather be shown by providing her with the tools to make her scrutiny effective and truth-revealing, perhaps by providing background information, or by stimulating her to stretch her mind and ruthlessly to think through to her conclusions. The aim will not be to produce a certain kind of end-result but to stimulate a certain kind of growth.

In a similar way, her sexuality is entering into a new phase of rapid development. In childhood, one may hope, the individual has begun learning how to love. Initially this is in response to the relationship proffered by its parents and later by its brothers and sisters, friends and teachers. Through these experiences it develops into an outgoing person, capable of unselfish relationships. Just as this precarious balance is achieved, however, a new element, conscious sexuality, appears, threatening to upset the applecart. In boys (but somewhat later in girls) the strength of the sexual urge reaches its peak very quickly, long before the personality has had time to readjust and integrate this new and wayward force. And like any other emotion, which is not properly under the control of the will, its tendency is selfish. The sexuality of the young adolescent is typically introspective. A boy is likely to be pre-occupied with his own sensations and may find in masturbation a normal expression at this stage. A girl is more likely to give way to a self-indulgent romanticism, often homosexual in content, or to experiment with her new-found power over the opposite sex. Judged by adult standards these activities may be wrong, disordered, deficient or what-you-will. By pubescent standards they are appropriate. Why should it cause any surprise—or for that matter moral indignation—for an immature person to react to a problem in an immature way?

A realistic acceptance of what adolescence means is not to sell the pass on moral values. On the contrary it makes the only foundation on which to stimulate constructive growth towards maturity. But the growth must be from the inside. Whoever heard of a gardener exhorting his trees to grow? And yet we cheerfully implore our adolescents to become grown up, and are hurt when they fail to do so immediately. No amount of cajoling or threatening can mature Josephine; like the tree this can only occur from inside, at her own pace and according to her own nature. And since this is human nature, she will only learn maturity in loving through the experience of loving and of being loved—just as she did as a child. Like her friends she gradually developed from inward-looking sexuality, expanding to take in the demands of sexually based relationships. At this particular stage she is learning, through hard experience, how the physical urge can run ahead of capacity for responsibility, precipitating her into a situation she is not yet ready to handle. She is aware that sexual intercourse is a significant action, but she is not quite sure whether this significance makes it inappropriate to her present relationship. She has yet to understand its function as the medium of the total self-giving of marriage both in sign and in expression. And this is not surprising. Before a person can understand what it means to give themselves totally, they must be able to possess themselves totally—which, after all, is what we mean by maturity, where human beings are concerned. And this gradual integration of self, under the control of the will, takes place through a self-knowledge and self-mastery in which the mistakes as much as the felicities of immaturity play their part.

It might seem that the best thing for an adult to do is to stand well back and hope that no explosion takes place. And there is truth in this, for nothing is more dangerous than clumsy fingers reaching into other people's souls. But, provided he respects the law of growth, the gardener can do a great deal to ensure that the tree reaches a proper maturity. The first need which an adolescent will often have is for someone who is prepared to listen. Good listening is not a passive ability but an active creative talent. With the help of a good listener a whole jumble of thoughts and emotions can be articulated into shape and, in their new form, be examined for true value. Sometimes the opportunity to stimulate the process is given and the listener can put forward questions that lead the young mind into unexplored avenues to correct an emphasis or discover a truth. Sometimes straight information will be required: this may be a reflection of human experience or a fact of which the person concerned is ignorant. But it must not be information to prove a point—rather it should be a facet of reality which should be taken into account in reaching a decision or forming an attitude. Everything should be approached from the perspective of the young person helping him to evaluate his experiences and develop from them towards the next stage.

When the blind lead the blind and they both fall into the pit, at least the damage is limited by the joint disaster. But when the sighted lead the blind, without an understanding of their blindness, only their charges are removed from the scene, while the enthusiastic helpers move blithely on to the next catastrophe. Human nature being what it is, a considerable self-discipline is required to avoid a situation where the adult is trying to impose his own views on the person he is attempting to help. From the standpoint of his maturity the attitudes of the young are clearly deficient and the urge to point this out can be almost irresistible. But to succumb to the urge is dangerous and self-defeating. The achievement of acceptance into the adult world through a veneer of the views of others, rather than through profound internal growth, is at the expense of remaining basically infantile long after the period nature has allotted for this process.

In fact the danger is only potential because the young have an excellent built-in 'fuse' which blows when damage is likely to be done. For example 'good advice' is rarely harmful because it is usually ignored. One might well argue that it would be unkind to deprive the well-meaning adult of the simple pleasure which his self-indulgence will give him. Likewise, continual suggestions —often tendered in a kindly and tolerant fashion—that the young person falls woefully short of the standards required for adult behaviour, usually fall safely on deaf ears. There are instances however where this can have the effect of suggesting to the young person that his particular inadequacies are insuperable, or that maturing is a process involving a single leap, a simple act of will. Finding this impossible he may give up the struggle or alternatively he may rationalize his frustration by elevating his deficiencies into virtues and believe he has achieved maturity in his contemptuous rejection of adult values.

Without doubt the biggest danger lies in the imposition of moral judgment. The fuse does not blow so easily here—the latent manicheism which is always ready to attach 'sin' to sexual disorder, combined with the legalistic frame which we build into the Catholic young, sees to that. The result can be a corrosive sense of false guilt, utterly destructive in its mordant effect which —all too often—brings about a stunting of normal growth towards sexual maturity. A second result, frequently combined with the first, is an escape from the dilemma by a complete rejection of religious values involving the cessation, perhaps for many years, of spiritual development. When I read of pupils at a Catholic school avoiding confession (as it is currently conceived) but making greater use of holy communion, I can only wonder at the providence of God which guides their sure instinct.[3]

The distinction here lies between the moral judgment which is imposed on other people—on which scripture looks askance[4]—and the moral judgment which we impose on ourselves. The young, in fact, have a very special contempt for wishy-washy adults who are unwilling to express their own moral convictions. But the essentially subjective nature of moral judgment must be respected. The fundamentals of this often complex process are straightforward. The individual compares his actions with the principles of good and evil behaviour which he recognizes to be true. But, quite plainly, he is the only person who knows what he recognizes as good or evil—no one can perform this function for him. Naturally he has the obligation to take appropriate steps to ensure that these principles are sound ones, but since he is an adolescent the normal methods of doing this are restricted by his situation. As I have suggested, a scepticism with regard to external authority is a natural and necessary element of the stage he has reached, and his capacity for the recognition of God's moral demands for order in the sexual sphere is impaired by the very immaturity which is the definition of his adolescence.

It is not immaturity which is sinful; this can only occur when, as Fr Schoonenberg points out, it is 'willed'.[5] Here the individual takes a deliberate stand against what he recognizes as his fulfilment as a human being. But this recognition itself implies an advance in maturity. St Paul's irony that connects the possibility of guilt with the advent of law is verified here.[6] In helping the young person towards an understanding of what God requires

[3] Dom David Bird, O.S.B., survey at Belmont Abbey School, *Catholic Herald*, 17 Jan. 1969. See also 'The Sacrament of Penance—An Investigation' and 'Confessional Practice (A Limited Survey)', *The Clergy Review*, February 1966 and October 1968 respectively.
[4] Luke 6 : 37 and Rom. 14 : 12-14.
[5] *Man and Sin*, Sheed and Ward, London, 1965, p. 42.
[6] Rom. 5 : 13.

of him, in the very stimulation of maturity that makes his subsequent actions a real moral choice, guilt becomes possible. But, and this is of crucial importance, it will not be a false guilt. A false guilt appears when a person feels he has done wrong without a full recognition of his fault or without full control over his actions. It is damaging because he can do nothing about it. He cannot be sorry, he has nothing to be sorry for. He cannot resolve amendment, there is nothing to amend. He cannot even make proper retribution, the debt was not his. True guilt, on the other hand, which results from the individual accepting that he chose to do something which he knew at the time was wrong, has a directly opposite effect. The appropriate response is contrition, amendment, restitution and—in my immediate context—sacramental forgiveness. Far from being of a negative quality it becomes a vital element of growth.

I have often thought that a suitable patron saint for adolescents would have been Blondin the tightrope walker. Although the punishment for error in his case would have been the relatively light one of dashing his brains out in Niagara Falls, progress through adolescence without falling foul of the comprehensive catalogue of sins carrying the price tag of eternal punishment, would seem to demand skills of a similar order. In such an atmosphere natural growth is not really possible. The adolescent needs a freedom to experiment, to discover and to understand. A married couple could not hope to develop authentic rich sexual expression of their love with a Vatican-approved checklist by their bed. They need to grow freely, preserving and enhancing what they find benefits their relationship and discarding what destroys. Provided their intention is to promote their love and to fulfil God's plan for them through it, sin does not arise.

Similarly for the adolescent. His fundamental moral direction is set by whether or not he is trying to move towards a real maturity in which he completes and fulfils his human nature. His glance should not be backwards but always forwards to deepening his understanding of himself and growing in self-possession. In this process his adult counsellors can play an important part, not by relieving him of the responsibility of growth, but by helping him to learn more fully from his experiences. In stimulating him to think through his attitudes and his choices and, in presenting to him aspects he had not taken into account, they can reflect a true picture of reality against which he can form himself. Their function will certainly not be to impute guilt: if he falls short of what was in his power to do he will impute his own. Indeed the counsellor may be more concerned to help him separate the true guilt from the false—the inspiration of the Spirit from that of the Liar, who was one from the beginning.

Josephine's problem was the introduction to this essay and its solution will make a fitting envoy. My wife, who actually does most of the work, on these occasions, invited her to express more fully the doubts which had brought her for advice in the first place. This led her to think about the overall value of her relationship and in doing so she clarified her concern about the speed at which it had progressed. She was then asked to consider whether her feelings for the young man were such that intercourse would be the right expression of them. Josephine could not make up her mind about this—and that brought the realization that, in such an emotional turmoil, she was not in a state to open a can of beans, let alone make a decision as profound as this one. And so she felt she had better postpone her rubicon until she could get the whole matter into perspective. As she was due to take up a place in a provincial university within a few days, she decided to carry out a 'holding operation' until her new environment gave her the chance to think things out. That evening she and her young man went to the cinema and said goodnight at the station.

What was gained? Perhaps nothing but a postponement—we shall probably not know. But it is possible that Josephine may have benefited. She may have learned something about the dangers of letting relationships intensify when there is no possibility of marriage. She will have seen very clearly how physical sexuality leads remorselessly towards its proper biological term. She will have learned something about herself within sexual relationship and her ability to transcend the apparently inevitable. In her more relaxed future consideration she may come to a more definite conclusion about the significance of sexual intercourse. She will undoubtedly get a new perspective on her young man's character in his reaction to her decision. Small gains, perhaps—but, where growth is concerned, speed is not of the essence. What matters is that it should be in the right direction.

4. Sex and Christian Loving
JOHN MARSHALL

SEX is a problem. How often have we heard that said or seen it written. We speak of sex as though it were some disease, like rheumatism, or some process, like aging, from which there is no escape. We think of it as something apart from ourselves, something alien to the real person we are. We do not think of it as an integral part of ourselves. But this is in fact what it is; we are men or we are women; there are no neuter beings in the human species. Our failure to recognize and accept this simple fact lies behind much of our difficulty about sex.

It is not surprising that we should think of sex as something alien. A generation of Catholics trained to react to the question, 'Of which must I take more care, of my body or of my soul?' with the reply 'I must take more care of my soul because...' cannot help but think of the body, not only as something separate from their real self, but also as something inferior. But the origin of our problem lies more deeply than a badly worded catechism question and answer. Cartesian dualism has contributed a great deal to our lack of understanding of our sexuality.

There is clearly great difficulty in explaining in philosophical terms what man is, nor is this the place to enter into this complex philosophical problem. It is sufficient for us to recognize that there is a problem concerning what is variously described as the mind-body or body-soul relationship. But difficult though the problem is, it does not help to proffer a solution which, simple though it may appear, raises more problems than it solves. To think of the body and soul as quite separate entities, the soul being the real man and the body a mere appendage, is just such a solution; and it has certainly clouded our understanding of our sexuality.

Though revelation has shed much light upon this problem, it has not solved all our difficulties. When God began his material creation, he did not create spirits which he then clothed in material cover. He said, 'Let us make man in our own image, in the likeness of ourselves' (Gen. 1 : 26) and, without any more ado, 'God created man in the image of himself, in the image of God he created him, male and female he created them,' (Gen. 1 : 27). Having done it, 'God saw all he had made, and indeed it was very good' (Gen. 1 : 31).

The earlier account of creation which is contained in the second chapter of Genesis takes us further into our origins. 'Yahweh God fashioned man of dust from the soil. Then he breathed into his nostrils a breath of life, and thus man became a living being,' (Gen. 2 : 7). From this we derive the idea of God infusing life into a particular ensemble of his material creation. There is no emphasis here upon duality. God made a material form and breathed into it the breath of life. This was man.

This biblical account of the creation of man shows him as a unity. The moment we divide him into body and soul, that moment we have lost him, we have in fact destroyed him. The moment the soul and body are separated in life, that same moment we recognize that man has died. It is true that we believe that he has not by death been annihilated. But the mode of his existence between death and resurrection is something we do not understand; nor has revelation shed light on this. What we do know is that after resurrection on the day of judgment we shall live on eternally as embodied beings as does Christ.

If then we want to think about man we have to think about that material form into which God breathed the breath of life. We cannot consider the soul without the body, nor the body without the soul if we want to consider man. Man is body and soul together and if we only have one, we do not have man. We certainly cannot attribute a problem to man's body and hope thereby to rid ourselves of the problem on the grounds that, because it is of the body, it does not concern the real man which is contained in the soul.

It may seem absurd to suggest that anyone would want to

dismiss a problem concerning man in this way. But this is precisely what we do with regard to sex. We attribute sex to the body; we separate the body as not being of the essence of man and so we deceive ourselves into thinking we have rid ourselves of the problem of sex. Of course we do not put it in so blunt a way, otherwise even those of us whose powers of self-deception are most highly developed could not shut our eyes to this absurdity. We are much more subtle about it than that. We recommend that the problem of sex should be solved by chastising the body, by mortifying the flesh and bringing it into subjection. We ask why married people are making so much fuss about the papal teaching on contraception. Can they not learn to develop a spiritual love between them? In this way we imply that something which was only of the spirit (were that possible) would be something of the real man. In these and other ways we show ourselves to be not only dualists, but also dualists with priorities. We reveal a scale of values which are the product, not of anything we have learned from God's revelation, but of our own distorted view of what he created which was in fact 'very good'.

To see more of God's plan concerning our sexuality we must return to the account in Genesis. God said, 'It is not good that the man should be alone' (Gen. 2 : 18). None of the forms of material creation that God had made was able to remedy this deficiency. So God made woman to be man's helpmate. 'That is why a man leaves his father and mother and joins himself to his wife, and they become one body' (Gen. 2 : 24).

This is the way that God created man and this is the way that we should see him. We are men or we are women. We are not basically indeterminate beings to whom male or female sexual organs are attached. We are not first human and then men or women. From the moment of our conception sexual differentiation has begun. It is true that man and woman are so closely related that biological and psychological influences can deviate us to a significant degree from our initial path, but our sexuality is with us from the moment of our conception. It is not something added later. It is with us because it is us.

Nor does our sexuality lie dormant until we reach the stage of puberty. It is manifest from the outset in differing susceptibility to disease, differing neonatal and infant mortality and different behaviour. Parents, the family, society reinforce this by the different attitudes they adopt towards boys and girls even as infants. The saying 'blue for a boy, pink for a girl' reflects the feeling that from the outset there is a difference between these two types of human being which we exploit and encourage in a thousand and one ways.

When, therefore, we talk about sexuality and Christian loving we are really talking about how men and women should love one another for there is no sex apart from persons; there is no maleness that is not part of a man and no femaleness that is not part of a woman. But before going on with this we must first consider what we mean by loving.

Love, being a much misused word, is frequently misunderstood. It expresses a complex notion at the centre of which is the idea of service. The giving of oneself in the service of another is the essence of love. Yet it is something more than service alone. If it were service alone, the word service would surely do to describe it. The paradox of love is that, though one is giving, one is at the same time receiving. Nor must the love be returned for this to happen. Unrequited love does not go without its reward. The giving of oneself in the service of another secures for oneself a new perspective, a new depth of understanding, a new dimension. It is under the influence of love that man flowers and matures in a way that no other experience produces. It is the intercommunion between beings, which is a part of love, that enables man to develop his maximum human potential. As God said, 'It is not good that the man should be alone' (Gen. 2 : 18). Man is a relational creature and develops the fulness of his being in relation to others.

Christ preached as his central theme just this kind of loving. 'Which is the greatest commandment of the law?' the pharisee asked (Mt. 22 : 36) and Christ told him it was to love, to love God and to love our fellow men. Love was to be the hallmark of the Christian : 'By this love you have for one another, everyone will know that you are my disciples,' said Christ (Jn 13 : 35).

This love was not to be a half-hearted affair. It was to be a full-blooded effort to serve to the best of one's ability. 'A man can have no greater love than to lay down his life for his friends' (Jn 15 : 13) was the standard to be set. It was not just a question of avoiding offending, or minimally serving; it was a matter of whole-hearted giving even to the point of life itself. And to show that he really meant it Christ did just that : he gave his life for his friends.

Why then is sex a problem? We have seen that sex is not something apart from us; it is us. We have seen that loving is the giving of ourselves to the service of another. All our loving is, therefore, sexual for we ourselves are sexual. Perish the thought! How could this possibly be when for years we have been taught to suppress the sexual, to purify our love and to cleanse it as far as possible of the dross of sexuality. How often have we been urged to elevate our love to the level of angels or, if we cannot make that high goal, at least to the level of 'brother and sister'. What a state of confusion lies here, much of it stemming from our dualistic conception of man as a being composed of body and soul, the soul being the real man. Man certainly has a body; he likewise has a soul. But man is not soul any more than he is body; man is body-soul. This is how God made him; that is how he is.

When man loves, therefore, he loves as a body-soul being. Man perceives the object of his love through his senses, he apprehends that object with his intellect, his will moves him towards it, he communicates with it through word and look, through gesture and touch. In other words it is as a man that he brings himself into relationship with the object of his love. And this man is not some inner being operating the body as the puppeteer operates his puppet on a string. The body-soul complex which comes into relationship with the other being is the man. The look, the gesture, the word, the touch are all manifestations of man loving. Equally the erection is no more and no less than this. It is man reaching out to another. It is because we fail to see this that we have so much difficulty with the 'problem of sex'. It is our habit of separating things of the body from things of the spirit which creates so many difficulties for us.

There may at first sight seem to be little in common between yesterday's manual of moral theology and pornography. Yet closer inspection shows that, though written with different intentions, they are in fact of a kind. It is not just that both are dealing with sex; it is their approach to sex which is the same. The most striking thing is that neither deals with people; both are content to describe acts in isolation from people. The pornographic book contains a predictable series of descriptions of bodily appositions in a predictable series of permutations; there are no people, only actions. Those to whom the actions are attached are vague silhouettes without any substance. The pornographic adventures set in London could equally well be in Brooklyn, Paris or Cairo; the story set in the twentieth century could equally well be in the eighteenth or nineteenth centuries; the involvement of people from one class of society could equally well apply to people of another class.

Yesterday's manual of moral theology is just the same. There are no people, only acts. These again are predictable in their pattern of complete and incomplete acts, natural and unnatural, in an endless series of categories and sub-categories. It is true that elsewhere in the theological writings man as man is considered, but nothing written there is allowed to contaminate the clear categorization of the moral manual. Intercourse is not primarily a relationship between two people, it is the deposition of true semen in the vagina. Not only is the body separated from the soul, but the genital parts of the body are separated from the remainder. We find ourselves dealing with genitalia in isolation, completely divorced from anything remotely resembling man.

The error and consequences of this approach are readily apparent. The evil portrayed by pornography becomes easy to see. It describes the use of one human being by another, the exploitation of one person by another. No regard is given to the person; the person is irrelevant; it could equally well be this person as that. All that matters is the body, which is used by another for private satisfaction. It is this, rather than the performance of some particular action, which is the real evil. Man is not being treated as man, a creature made in the image and likeness of God. Man is being treated merely as a convenient instrument through which a personal satisfaction may be gained and a desire assuaged.

Man in this situation is not treated with the reverence which is proper to him. We often have a false idea about reverence. We see it as an external attitude such as joining our hands to pray, bowing our head at the consecration or genuflecting to kiss the bishop's ring. And often the external attitude bears little relationship to our internal feelings. Reverence is really respect for a person because of what he is. Man is a person made in the image and likeness of God. We reverence him (the whole of him, that is, body and soul), not because to use him for fornication is against the rules, but because to do so is to fail grossly to respect something of God which is in reality unique and very precious. Pornography is evil, not because it describes actions which are against the rules, but because it portrays a complete loss of respect for the person, a total failure to respect him as a human being.

The manual of moral theology, though its intentions are different, ends up in the same situation. Respect for persons is lost sight of in the minutiae of physical actions. The description of actions divorced from persons gives the idea that it is with actions and not with people that this theology is concerned. The question, 'How far can we go?' expresses very clearly this mentality. What actions can we indulge in without transgressing the rules? Actions, not people, all along the line. The effect of this approach is to lower standards rather than to raise them, to debase man, not to elevate him. Any theology of sex which is not a theology of the entire man misses the point.

The suggestion that the theology of sex should get rid of its preoccupation with bodily actions and concentrate upon the whole man is always met with the objection that this is to abandon objective morality. The upholders of this view contend that they are not in fact concerned with the body alone; they point to chapters elsewhere in their manual, chapters which deal with the factors which influence a human act, ignorance, fear, habit, overwhelming passion and so on. They declare that this is evidence enough that their concern is not exclusively with the body, that they do consider the whole man. But their protests do not convince.

Recent discussion on contraception has revealed this only too clearly. The idea that an act in which sperm and ovum were prevented from meeting could be creative seemed to them a paradox because they looked at the act solely in bodily terms. They saw the essentials of the marriage act as being the deposition of true semen in the vagina. They saw the essence of the contract as being the exchange of rights over one another's bodies for acts apt for generation. Of course, they granted that there should be love there as well, but this was peripheral rather than central, accidental rather than essential. They protested that if you take away the essential criterion of deposition of true semen in the vagina, then you have abandoned objective morality and are in situation ethics in which every act is simply what the person intends it to be. This is, of course, not so. The error comes from confusing objective with material or, in the case of sex, with bodily. But non-material things are just as objective as are material.

This tendency to equate objective with material and to confuse external observable actions with truly human acts is nothing new. Christ encountered the same situation two thousand years ago when the Pharisees objected that his disciples ate without first washing their hands. 'Listen, and understand,' he said, 'What goes into the mouth does not make a man unclean; it is what comes out of the mouth that makes him unclean' (Mt. 15 : 10). Then he went on to list these as 'murder, adultery, fornication, theft, perjury, slander' (Mt. 15 : 19). Likewise, following the sermon on the mount he declared, 'You have learnt how it was said: "You must not commit adultery." But I say this to you: "If a man looks at a woman lustfully, he has already committed adultery with her in his heart." ' (Mt. 5 : 27-28). In this way Christ made it very clear that morality cannot be described solely in terms of bodily acts; the whole man is involved and it is what *he* does not what *his body* does that matters.

Those who fear that objective morality is being abandoned

find great difficulty in seeing what criteria of morality can be laid down, especially in the genital sphere, if there is no strict embargo on certain bodily actions as such. Why should a man not show his love for his fiancée by giving himself to her in intercourse if the act in itself is not wrong? Would it not be sufficient then to say that his intention was to manifest love in order to justify whatever action he chose to perform? If his intention is to love, what does it matter how he shows his love. It is putting the question in this way which reveals the separation of soul and body and the preoccupation with the latter that is at the root of the problem. If the body is not to be the criterion, then the only other possible criterion for those who hold this view is intention and this would be situation ethics. But we are not in fact forced to choose between these alternatives once we learn to see man as he really is. It is because we separate body and soul that we find ourselves faced with what is in fact a false antithesis. The question is what the man as a whole does. What is the totality of the act in which he, as the body-soul complex which he is, indulges? It is not enough to say that his intention was this or that; equally it is not enough to say that his body did this or that; nor is it enough to say that his body did this and then to introduce a number of factors, such as ignorance, fear, habit and so on, to qualify what is regarded as the essential act.

Seeing man as a totality involves no loss of objectivity in moral criteria. The criteria are, in fact, more rigorous, more exacting. Let us take the act of intercourse as an example. Human sexual intercourse is not just depositing semen in the vagina. It is a more elevated human act than that. Intercourse is an expression, a sign, of the total giving of one person to another. It is not an act which involves only the genital organs; it engages the entire human person. This is why it can only properly take place in the monogamous, indissoluble marriage, and there can only properly be performed as an expression of love.

What happens in pre- or extra-marital intercourse? Let us leave aside those who are merely using their partner for some physical or psychological satisfaction, as a step towards their own maturity or as a means of sorting out their own confusion. Let us concentrate on those who are truly manifesting some degree of love. There may well be a degree of giving in this situation, but it is not, it cannot be, the total giving of the marital act because the two people have not as yet seen fit to make that dedication of themselves to each other. They may declare that they would indeed make this dedication but circumstances prevent it; his wage is not enough, they have not got a place to live, she must finish her studies. But the very fact that these circumstances impede them shows that either they are unable, or unwilling, at this point in time to make that commitment to each other which is involved in marriage. In these circumstances to perform the act which is a sign, a symbol, an expression of that commitment is a contradiction. The person is saying—as we do say through bodily acts—what he does not truly mean, hence the act is wrong. This is every bit as objective as any criterion based on mere anatomy or physiology; indeed, it is more so for it involves the objective criterion of the whole man.

Nor does the argument that if contraception were no longer held to be intrinsically evil, there would be no grounds for condemning premarital intercourse, provided one hundred per cent efficient contraception were used, have validity. This also reflects the preoccupation with the bodily aspects of the act. This argument says in fact, 'Change the biological character of the act and you have changed the nature of the act'. This is not really so because the act is something more than is contained in its biological aspect alone; it is an intercommunication between two persons, an expression of meaning and it is in this total context that it must be assessed. What is the totality of this act?

Love is to give, to give oneself in the service of another. This is a form of communication matched by no other in the experience of man. The giving of oneself means that the body-soul complex is involved. There cannot be communication without the body, at least in the state in which we are now. Love must be expressed by look, word, gesture, touch. Christ appreciated this full well so that when he wished to provide for continued communication with man after his ascension he created the eucharist so that man would come into contact with Christ in a tangible form.

We can see from this how misleading is talk of 'spiritual' love or the 'spiritual' life. The idea that man can develop a truly human love for God without involving his whole self is completely erroneous. Attempts to do this often result in the individual, far from reaching out towards God, turning in upon himself in the mistaken belief that there he is finding God. The communion between himself and Christ in the eucharist in the old liturgy, with its emphasis on the bowed head and the private prayer, was often a self-comforting procedure rather than a giving of himself to God. There is for man no spiritual life as such; there is only human life as God gave it. This life involves the whole man; it engages the totality of his body-soul complex; it is to this complex that God has extended his invitation to which man should respond fully as man.

The error of concentrating on what was called the spiritual life is matched by the opposing error of being busy about many things as was Martha, but of having no time for God. This error comes about not only by the conscious rejection of God, as in the humanist approach, but also by the over-preoccupation with man.

The response of man to God involves a response of man to his fellow men. 'A man who does not love the brother that he can see cannot love God, whom he has never seen' (1 Jn 4 : 20). This love of fellow men also involves the entirety of man, the entirety of his body-soul complex. It makes a man give himself in the service of another, a giving which he manifests through his bodily actions. It is through the acts that man performs that he manifests himself to another. 'You will be able to tell them by their fruits' (Mt. 7 : 20).

But this man to whom the service is given is the creature made in the image and likeness of God, sharing with God the divine gifts that God has bestowed upon him, participating in the divine life through grace and through being a part of the mystical body of Christ. It is for this reason that one man gives service to another, for in serving man he is serving God. If he loses sight of this, becoming so preoccupied with the needs of man that he loses sight of God and makes mankind itself a God, then he has lost his true goal. Seeing God beyond man does not mean that the person must do less for man, that he must limit his service to man in order to have time for God. It means that in serving man he must constantly see the God who is in, yet beyond, the man. And because human memory requires constant reminders if it is not to forget, man must pray; he must constantly communicate with God so that he does not lose sight of him in the crowd of men he is endeavouring to serve for God's sake.

Many people, seeking what they consider to be their maximum human development and what they call the totality of human experience in order that they may become fully human, deceive themselves. They enter into a relationship with another person initially with the idea of giving service. But in that giving they also receive. The satisfaction they thereby obtain may lead them to lose sight of the God that dwells in the person yet beyond him. They then begin to exploit the other, using them as a stepping-stone towards an allegedly greater maturity. The fact that each may be using the other in this way does not excuse the conduct of either the one or the other, for no man has the right to use another in this way. Man belongs to God, not to his fellow men.

The tendency that man undoubtedly has to exploit others in this way is often attributed to a disorder in the sexual sphere. We know from revelation of the fall of man but it is a gratuitous assumption that the fall primarily involved disorder in the sexual sphere. In fact, as we have seen, man's sexuality cannot be separated from man himself. Man's fall did not therefore involve his sexuality alone; it could not, it had to involve the entirety of man. By viewing man as a whole we are not losing sight of the reality of the fall and its consequences. We are not living in a dream world where all is perfect and refusing to accept that there can be and is evil in the world. But evil is not of the body, as Christ pointed out. Evil is of the totality of man. And just as evil is of the totality of man, so is good. Sexuality is of the totality of man, hence there is no paradox between sexuality and Christian loving.

Moral theology has been dominated by a concern with bodily acts for so long that it is hard for many people to think in any other terms, especially in the so-called sexual sphere. In fact many are quite unable to do so; for others it might be possible, but they fear to take the step lest in doing so they find themselves adrift without anything to replace what they regard as the objective criteria they presently have. The future of marriage in the Christian context demands a vast new theological effort. Present problems cannot be solved by juggling with categories which the advances of theological and scientific knowledge have shown to be unreal. Nor can the task be performed by professional theologians working alone. It must be shared by others whose knowledge and experience provide data vital to the proper completion of this task. These include not only experts in other disciplines but also married people themselves who by reflection upon and discussion of their experience can contribute greatly to our knowledge.

This knowledge needs to be collected and collated. In this task marriage advisory councils have an important part to play. Their corporate experience of marriage, not only pathological through their reconciliation work, but also normal through their educational work with groups of all kinds, gives them a unique opportunity to serve the advancement of knowledge and understanding. By pooling their experience, and by objective appraisal of what it teaches, they can play an important part in the task that lies ahead.

This is a great challenge to the Church at the present time. Our theology of the relationships of men and women, particularly in marriage, has been a greatly neglected field. Criteria of judgment have been applied without any real understanding of the state to which they were being applied. Current technological advances may seem to be provoking new questions in relation to marriage. Our difficulty in answering these questions arises, not so much from the far-reaching nature of the advances, but from the inadequacy of our understanding of marriage itself. The time is ripe for a new advance. The way in which we respond to this challenge will have as great a bearing on the future happiness of mankind as will his control of nuclear weapons or his landing on the moon.

5. *Married and Other Loves*
PATRICIA MARSHALL

MARRIAGE, the priesthood and Christianity have all to do with love. What I want to do here is to look through love to marriage and, from marriage, reflect on Christianity and the priesthood.

Love
Since marriage is—or should be—a relationship of love it has certain things in common with any love relationship. One cannot really talk about love without talking about relationship, because love has no existence apart from persons—living persons relating to each other with all that this implies. One might for example remember or admire or respect some long-dead historical figures but could not in any useful sense of the phrase talk about a love relationship with them. If God were not a living and personal God then, for me anyway, the love of God would need to be redefined.

If love is personal, then human love must be sexual. We are all sexed persons. This is not to say that all love relationships involve the aim or desire for sexual intercourse or for homosexual practice. It does mean that there is a difference between the love of a woman for another woman and her love for a man, the difference being precisely a sexual one. We all learn this early in life from the different kind of relationship we have with our father and with our mother. Part of this difference is probably a matter of differing personalities but a large element in this is the fact that one of these is the same sex as ourselves and the other the opposite sex. We see it also in the love relationships of Christ—

his relationship with John, the beloved disciple, with Mary Magdalen, with the whole family at Bethany—Christ was wholly a man and loved them as a man. I am not sure if the current jargon phrase 'personal encounter with Christ' means anything but, if it does, then it should presumably mean that there would be a difference in the love of a man and the love of a woman for Christ, the man.

Love involves knowing and being known. At the minimum this means there must be some communication between the people involved. The communication, the Word, of God was made flesh in Christ in order that we might know him. If we are going to love, going to accept love, this means there must be some giving and accepting between us; this will be expressed in continuing communication, in service, even in sacrifice, the initial opening out in love towards another which is charity. But this kind of opening out involves the risk of being hurt, which is why love is difficult, why we constantly retreat into our self-made shells where we are safe and invulnerable; the extent to which we love is the extent to which we are prepared to let ourselves be vulnerable to another. We can never, in human relationships, have a guarantee that we will not be hurt; we could not, dare not, put ourselves in this position unless we had some hope that we might survive undestroyed. And this hope, justified by experience, is what leads us to trust another person, to have faith in them. To trust and be trusted which means to take responsibility for ourselves, for them, for our relationship and all that that involves. I think it is usually this way round in human relationships: from knowledge to love, through hope to faith. Is this true also of Christ and the Church? Are we given the gift of faith because through knowledge we have loved and through love learned to hope, rather than loving because we have been given the gift of faith?

Whichever way round it is, when we have learnt to love and to be loved in this kind of way, at however minimal a level, then this relationship has the possibility of being creative and developing for the people involved. All love relationships should be creative since they 'create' first of all the people who love.

Marriage

This then is true of all love relationships, at differing levels depending on the closeness, the depth, of the relationship. What is different about marriage? What distinguishes it from any other man-woman love relationship? Essentially, I think, it is totality. Acceptance and giving here are prepared to be *total*. In the marriage service we pledge ourselves to accept not only the geographical total of each other in the commitment of our bodies to each other but also the historical total 'for better or worse, till death'. Whatever we are, whatever we may become, is given and accepted totally. The pledge is made in the marriage service, the actuality is expressed in the total communicating gesture of sexual intercourse. (Incidentally, this is why I think sexual intercourse in a context which is not total is wrong: because it is 'saying' something which is not true.) But sexual intercourse not only symbolizes and expresses this relationship, it also develops it, moves it on. The expression 'to make love' in reference to intercourse is a good one because this is just what it does—or can do. This is true of any loving communication. I may love you but when I tell you, in words or in gesture, that I love you, this not only expresses a truth but also moves the relationship on.

This kind of totality also involves, in a particular way, exclusiveness. A wife, involved in this total relationship with her husband, is not available to be someone else's wife, to be involved in the same total relationship with another. This does not mean, however, that she is not free to love anyone else. If anything, the reverse should be the case. Most marriages, I think, do need a period of in-turning, a time in which husband and wife may need to withdraw to some extent from the community to learn about each other and about themselves. (It is at this point that societies of various kinds start complaining that they cannot keep their young married members.) The danger, however, is that the couple remain here, content with the security that their love provides for each other but never progressing beyond this to turn out in love to the wider community. There can be, in marriage, and in any relationship a kind of 'ourselfishness' which is more corrosive than the usual 'myselfishness' because it masquerades as unselfishness.

The usual starting-point for an extension of the loving community beyond the couple themselves would be towards their own children but here again the same kind of 'ourselfishness' can envelop and enclose the family and be sanctified and enshrined in such phrases as: 'Charity begins at home', 'We are good neighbours, we keep ourselves to ourselves. We don't bother anyone else.' And how tragically limited this can become. Marriage and the community both lose if the couple and the family remain enclosed.

Married love should not be constricting. In the security of her husband's love for her, a wife recognizes herself as a woman, recognizes at once her worth and her unworthiness. In this recognition she can turn out in love towards others. It is, in a sense, with her husband's love that she does so. His creative love for her makes her what she is, his supportive love strengthens her in loving others. In the end we find that the exclusiveness of married love is very limited and that, apart from this limited sense, husband, wife and children are all 'for sharing'.

Christianity

Before looking at what marriage can teach us about Christ and the Church there is something which perhaps should be said. No Christian would deny that in terms of importance the precept 'love God' comes before 'love your neighbour'; but in practice for many people the order is chronologically reversed. Some, I think, do love God first, or at least seem to proceed straight from an understanding of love gained from their parents to a love of God through which they learn to love their neighbour. Others can only, and sometimes dimly, reach towards the love of God through a love of their neighbour, through a recognition of the 'otherness', the God-dimension, beyond the perceived reality. Married people, especially happily married people, are more likely because of their experience of this particular relationship to be in the second category. Are celibates more likely to be in the first? I am not sure, but if they are then it may present a difficulty when one group talks to the other about love of God. What I say, then, about Christianity must be seen in this light. For me, it is neighbour first and clearly, God through this and dimly.

Christianity is about love so that all that was said about love in general applies. But married love and Christianity have also in common the added dimension of totality. This applies not merely in terms of Christ's total commitment to the Church but also in terms of his invitation to us to make a similarly total commitment to him. There is a similarity between being received into the Church and being married. In each case one accepts an unknown future and for life. One cannot really have a trial marriage. One might try out sexual intercourse or keeping house together but one cannot try out permanence. In the same way one might attend Mass; one might even, provided it went unnoticed, receive the sacraments; but one cannot try out the permanence of a commitment to Christ. This total pledge of love is made an actuality in the eucharist: the physical expression of Christ's love for the Church, as intercourse is the physical expression of the love of husband and wife—the parallel here, I think, is remarkably close. Just as a wife is not meant to be passively submitting to intercourse, so the gesture of Christ in the eucharist invites a loving response from his Church.

Sexual intercourse, even in the best of marriages, will be a variable experience, not always up to concert standard. And though the invitation of Christ remains constant, our response may be less than adequate; it may require an effort on our part, but the effort should be the effort of love rather than a dreary routine duty. And as intercourse is not merely a statement of love but 'makes love', so the eucharist is and does the same. In both cases, though technique is of importance, too great a concentration on technique can be disastrous. What is important is to see how far each is an expression of love and a making of love.

What was said about exclusiveness in marriage applies also in the same limited way to Christianity. If I am committed to Christ, I am not available to be so committed to Mohammed or Kali. Do people in the same way need a period of in-turning, of intense concentration, here? Is this the point of the kind of private, intense celebrations of the eucharist in which one can positively feel the sense of community? And is there a similar danger here that these can be an end rather than a beginning? Are we content that we can have this kind of celebration for ourselves or are we prepared to use what we have learnt in order to share this love with a less coherent community, for example in a parish? As in marriage, the point of the love of God is to enable us to love others. His creative love makes us what we are; his supportive love strengthens us in loving others. In this way we come to recognize our other kinds of unity with other Christians, with other religions, with other human beings.

The priesthood and celibacy

In discussing the priesthood I am putting together two themes which are distinct; I recognize this confusion and make no apology for it. What we have at present is a celibate priesthood and, though I cannot personally see any reason why the priesthood should be exclusively celibate, I cannot see how we could do without celibacy altogether. Marriage needs celibacy. These two signs of love need each other and enrich each other. It has been said that marriage is the sign of God's love for each of us, the priesthood the sign of God's love for all of us. I am not sure whether this is helpful or just clever, but I offer it to you for what it is worth. They need each other especially in clarifying what each is. If there were only married and unmarried, the understanding of marriage would be more difficult. If celibacy is despised or misunderstood by the married, married love can easily become self-centred. Where marriage is despised or underrated by the celibates dedicated virginity is similarly diminished. Married and celibate alike must give witness to their vocation and must do so with their lives, recognizing not only the strength, but the fragility, of their vocation. The happily married must know what an offence their marriage is to those less fortunate. The priest similarly. The more cautious, perhaps more insightful, will recognize from the outset the fragility of the vocation. The more recklessly generous may need to be brought slap up against it, perceiving it like Peter, painfully, in the crowing of the cock.

Marriage needs also the irresponsibility of the responsible celibate. Married people and especially parents become so easily involved in compromise, the daily compromise that is so insidious. How can the parent, responsible for his children's welfare, 'sell all that he has and give to the poor'? He certainly cannot. It would probably be irresponsible for him to do so. But the celibate, because he has not this responsibility, can do this; he can not merely point to the counsels of perfection but live them, reminding the married not to be corroded by compromise.

But if we want celibacy—and I do—then we have a responsibility, all of us, for the celibate. The celibate priest, lacking the love of a wife through which to turn outwards in love to the whole community, must find his own spiritual centre from which to operate. He needs nevertheless to love and to be loved. The call to the priesthood is now as much as in earlier days a call to martyrdom—without any of the glamour that the idea, though not the actuality, of martyrdom may have held. A priest lays down his life for his friends. Do his friends love him for this? Do we show our love for our priests by putting them on a pedestal and chaining them to it? We give them the title Reverend and it is proper that we should show reverence to them as to any other (especially any other baptized) human being. But does this help to let them achieve the ordinary, warm, affectionate, human response we expect from our non-priest friends? One must be careful here of confusing technique with reality, but is it not an extraordinary thing that in situations of friendship in which we would have long since dropped the title had it been Mr or Dr, we continue to retain the title Fr for priests? Quite obviously in itself it makes little difference to a particular relationship whether a priest is addressed as Fr Smith or John; I merely remark on it as a symptom of the kind of relationship we seem to expect of priests. The priest lays down his life for his friends and is thereafter totally at the service of the community of which he is a part. If this is so, then a large part of the discussion about whether particular functions are proper to the role of the priest is irrelevant. The priest will do whatever is most needed of him by the community and whatever helps, not only to maintain, but to form and to build community. This at times may involve him in being a teacher, a doctor, a social worker or a bus-driver. None of this matters, provided it does not hamper the central function of the exercise of his priesthood.

The central function of the priesthood, as I see it, is to bring the Word of God to the community. The priest will do this in various ways. Obviously he will do this in the sacraments of which he is the minister, equally obviously in preaching. But I think we sometimes have a very limited understanding of what preaching is, thinking of it only as pulpit sermons. The Word was made flesh and dwelt amongst us in Christ. The priest makes the Word flesh again, not only in the eucharist, not only in preaching God's word from the pulpit like Christ in the sermon on the mount, and not only in his love and service of others like Christ in his healing ministry. Was the Word made flesh most clearly in the Sermon on the Mount or in healing, or was it still more powerfully made clear in the Garden, or when, broken and humiliated, he cried out to the God who seemed to have forsaken him? The priest preaches in his person, not only in his radiant joyful love of us, not only in the exemplary dedication of his life, but perhaps more than ever when weak, broken and humiliated he looks to us for support. And this applies not only to 'lovable' weaknesses but also to the less attractive, like aggressiveness, overbearing pompousness and deadly boringness.

The present situation in the Church could, if seen in human terms only, lead to despair. The millennium is not yet here, nor is it just around the corner. The Christian cannot be other than an optimist. He must believe that the Holy Spirit will operate. The Christian vocation for all is the same, a vocation to love, a vocation that will take a variety of forms. Whatever form it takes for us, whether married or yet-to-be married, whether dedicated virgins or single in the world, we must not lose faith in the Holy Spirit, must not feel that we have to take a hand and do his work for him, but recognizing our own frailty we must continue, however inadequately, bearing one anothers burdens and building the community of the sons and daughters of God.

6. Christian Marriage and Christian Unity

GORDON R. DUNSTAN

THE Church of England, when true to its tradition, is unsparing in the conceptual and theological demands which it makes on its people. Morning Prayer, for instance, in the old Book of Common Prayer, is as demanding an intellectual exercise as any Church could offer: and this the Church of England has offered for four centuries in village churches as well as in cathedrals. Similarly, the Form of Solemnization of Matrimony, in its first long sentence, calls on the congregation to see in the bride and bridegroom standing before them a sign pointing to the most profound theological mystery this side of the resurrection, namely 'the mystical union that is betwixt Christ and his Church'. And this for every marriage: not only for the marriages of theologians and ecclesiastics. The Common Prayer of the Church sets before the Church, at such decisive moments in the lives of its sons, the faith by which the Church lives: it demands a response to what is so given, an acceptance of the vision.

So in a Reformation formulary, drawn when the the visible unity of the Western Church was breaking—when marriage, because it was a subject of such controversy, was itself written, argued and preached about too often in the language of contumely and abuse—a vision of unity was embedded: marriage, like holy baptism and holy communion, is a *signum exhibitivum*, a sign of the continual presence of Christ in covenanted union with his Church, a visible witness to a Person and a relationship unseen. So did the Church of England affirm its adherence to the Christian tradition, building this insight of St Paul's again and again into the fabric of its marriage liturgy. It is nothing new for us to see in Christian marriage a sign of Christian unity.

Yet Christ makes all things new. In the ecumenical movement the sign is renewed; the jewel is burnished, so as to gleam again with forgotten splendour. Or so it would seem to theologians. The vision is not so clear everywhere. The barriers to sight are real, whether ecclesiastical, canonical, social, political, 'racial' or economic; and they are not removed simply by wishing them away. Ulster in the winter of 1968-69 must have been a very sad place for a man and woman, the one a Roman Catholic the other a Protestant, contemplating marriage together. There the theological and even ecclesiastical issues are lost in political issues. The political issues themselves are felt the more because they press painfully upon people's social and economic lives, and because they have historical depth: actual sufferings, actual injustices, past as well as present, can be evoked to inflame political passion. The language of religion becomes mere language, used with inflammatory intention and effect. If a mixed marriage is to be considered as a sign of the coming ecumenical unity, it must be considered in such a context as Northern Ireland, as much as in Southern France or any other region favoured with cultural homogeneity.[1] A certain realism is required, therefore, in contemplation and discussion: even if theological and ecclesiastical difficulties were at once dissolved, there would remain regions where the contracting of marriages between persons of differing Church allegiance presents difficulties which should not be underrated.

The difficulties, moreover, do not always disappear with marriage. When a mixed marriage falters, 'religion' can all too easily give occasion for the quarrels, and provide their weaponry. But religion is probably not the cause. The religion of each partner was part of a culture, part of what was familiar in childhood, of what comes to the surface again when emotions are disturbed. An Irish Catholic wife quarrelling with her English Protestant husband may have seething inside her a longing for all that culture

---

[1] 'La pastorale des foyers mixtes', *Aujourd'hui*, Journal de Taizé, 12 Nov. 1965. René Beaupère OP, 'Joint Pastoral Care', *Theology*, LXX, June 1967, p. 257.

which was her childhood home; her religion seems the more precious to her because it is part of that—and to him it is the more repellent for the same reason, when he is repelling her.

It is the duty of Churches, not to exacerbate these differences by aligning ecclesiastical allegiance with cultural and political frontiers, but by pastoral provision to secure an understanding of them, before marriage and in marriage, and so to help in the building of a true and stronger unity out of forces which otherwise might divide.

Two other tendencies can put mixed marriages out of focus. The first, still latent even in an ecumenical age, is to project the guilt of ecclesiastical division upon two people marrying across it. Samson took to wife a daughter of the Philistines; and while we still play at Israelites and Philistines in our Churches, the girl from the other side for whom our boy falls is all too easily cast in Delilah's role; her people are not as our people, her faith not our faith—she is a potential threat to the purity of our ways. So we legislate against her: we make her forsake her ways and embrace ours; if we fail, we attach conditions which, we hope, will protect our son, and, of course, the children. We make things difficult at the wedding: it must be different, somehow, from the wedding of two of 'our own'—otherwise people will not understand that we really disapprove, and others will follow their example. Then we watch them, waiting for the worst: we submit articles to the professional journals on 'the pastoral care of mixed marriages', so making of them a special case. We watch: we dare not let him slumber, his head in her lap, her hand toying with his hair: the lords of the Philistines are behind the door.

This is caricature; but caricature is reality overdrawn; and no one seriously engaged in discussion between the Churches on the problem of mixed marriages can fail to see the reality of *fear*, using regulation, law, as a protection. The Protestant fears the stereotypes, examined and unexamined, which he entertains about the Roman Catholic, and *vice versa*. And to the young who are in love and want to marry there is nothing to fear, nothing which they believe they cannot overcome, if they are allowed to try; and the regulations are, to them, so many petty hindrances upon their way. This is one tendency, one habit of mind, which puts the mixed marriage out of focus.

The second is its reverse. It is a symptom of toxic ecumenicity. It idealizes the mixed marriage, projects upon it all our unrealized hopes; it uses the couple like binoculars, to bring the distant event nearer—the day, the far-off *eschaton* when true unity (as they say) shall be achieved and all will be one. Did not Boaz of Bethlehem marry Ruth the Moabitess, and was not their son Obed, the father of Jesse, the father of David? And we all know who came of David's line. So the mixed marriage is an active symbol, an effective sign, of the end of our alienation; henceforth we can live as though our difficulties are resolved, and so they will be resolved. So again we make of the mixed marriage a special case. And we watch it, looking for signs, the sign of the Son of Man in the visible unity of his Church. We forget the sign of Jonah.

This too is caricature; but there is reality in it, the reality of unreflecting optimism which, while recoiling from the real difficulties, reduces the essentially flesh-and-blood stuff of marriage to a pseudo-theological symbol.

Now it is simply bad for people to see themselves and their marriage as a special case, or to be so regarded whether in dread or in holy adulation. Their being of different confessions is probably an accident in their relationship, one of the things they found out about one another when they began to take themselves seriously as candidates for marriage. If so, their first impulse is to regard it as an irritant to be assuaged, to be put beyond consciousness. If they are weak in their faith, they can take the path of indifference: conform to whatever is required of them in order to be married in the church of their choice, and then forget the whole thing. If one partner is weak and the other strong, the marriage may limp along on this uneven footing. Or one rather stronger may win over the one rather weaker, to join his Church: then we see unity by absorption—a model for our ecumenical future of which only the more tactless now talk aloud. In all this the mixed marriage differs not one jot from the great majority of marriages in a society widely indifferent to the active pursuit of Christian worship.

The issues begin to become clear only when the strong marries the strong, Samson (so to speak) with a lioness in another faith. When this happens, Churches have duties towards that marriage strictly prescribed by the theology of marriage which they teach: that is, they must respect that marriage in its integrity, in its totality; they may not exploit it, even for ecumenical purposes; they must not put stumbling blocks in its path, lest they incur the guilt of any division which they may provoke; they must serve it, with a service appropriate to its needs and governed finally by the end for which the marriage exists—the bringing of the spouses to the vision of God; and, recognizing the place that God has given to human freedom in his economy of salvation, they must respect in the marriage a freedom *not* to be served, the freedom even to shut the door. This is hard doctrine for Churches; but only in the terms of it can any solution of the ecclesiastical 'problem' of mixed marriages be found.

The 'problem' exists at two points: at the making of the marriage, and in the living of the married life. The contracting of mixed marriages is at present governed, for Roman Catholics, by the Instruction *Matrimonii Sacramentum*, issued from the Vatican on 18 March 1966. There is a strong possibility that, before this chapter is published, the Instruction will have been superseded by another; there is no point, therefore, in dwelling on its inadequacies or glossing its provisions. The new instruction, if it comes, should reflect the result of conversations between the Vatican Secretariat for Christian Unity and a group convened by the World Council of Churches;[2] and the work of a sub-commission of the Commission on Anglican-Roman Catholic Relations, the two meetings of which (to date) have been reported in the Vatican Secretariat's *Information Service* bulletins. A typical official Anglican response to the existing Roman Catholic regulations may be read in *Mixed Marriages between Anglicans and Roman Catholics*, by John G. Williams;[3] but this too, it is hoped, will be superseded if the new instruction is satisfactory.

---

[2] *Marriage and the Division among the Churches*, Geneva, World Council of Churches, 1967 (offprint from *Study Encounter*, III, 1).

[3] With a Foreword by the Archbishop of Canterbury. SPCK, 1967.

Other provinces in the Anglican Communion make their own provisions; but they do not differ widely in content from those in England. Meanwhile the journals carry responsible and thoughtful attempts to clarify the issues, and to secure that they are respected in whatever new regulations may be made.[4] It is beyond the purpose of this essay to pursue the question in all its particularity; only such aspects of it as are directly relevant to Christian unity are within the assignment made by the editor.

Ecclesiastical regulations, from whatever source they come, must respect the first theological principle, that holy baptism, by conferring Christian status and incorporating the new member into the body of Christ, is the indestructible bond of union between Christians and Christ, and so of Christians one with another.[5] A baptized man and woman entering upon a mixed marriage, therefore, are already members of a unity which transcends all ecclesiastical division. Discussions about 'reunion' have all too often forgotten this fundamental fact. Christians have much to be ashamed of in the historical processes which produced their present disorganization, and in the conduct of Churches one towards another. But they can be provoked by a carping world into professing shame for too much : their liturgical and cultural diversity, for instance, now in the process of high-minded but too rapid destruction, should be a cause of thankfulness for the vitality of the Spirit, not of shame. The unity which we seek ought not to require of us a cultural uniformity. Questions of organization and especially of Church order are more complicated because, while Anglicans and Roman Catholics comprehend within their

[4] E.g.: *Istina*, 1967, no. 2 (avril-juin), Franz Böckle *et al. Concilium*, VIII. 4, Oct. 1968, Ladislas Örsy SJ. *Hungarian Church Press*, XIX. 22, Nov. 1967, 'Conference on the Problems of Mixed Marriages'. *Lumière et Vie*, 87, mars-avril, 1968, 'Recommandations de l'Eglise catholique et des Eglises réformées et luthériennes de France pour la pastorale commune des foyers mixtes'. *One in Christ*, 1968, no. 2 and 1969, no. 1. *Theology*, LXX, 564, June, 1967 (editorial and three articles, one written by Rev. Maurice O'Leary, to whom the author of this chapter is deeply indebted for his understanding and appreciation of the Roman Catholic teaching and living of family life); LXXII, 584, Feb. 1969 (editorial). Cf. Mgr Henry G. J. Beck, of Lyndhurst, N.J., 'Proposed Pastoral Guidelines for Inter-Christian Marriages', read at Detroit, 1968.
[5] Cf. the Vatican II Decree on Ecumenism, I, 2.

respective professions similar theological understandings of the apostolic and episcopal character of the sacred ministry, they differ in the theological status which they give to the See of Rome: Anglicans do not confess that it is *essential* for the Church to be constituted in the communion of the Roman See—desirable as full communion with Rome would be. These differences are real. They do not break, however, and cannot break, the unity in Christ constituted by holy baptism; and this unity all regulations for marriage must respect.

Secondly, both Churches would confess that the essence of Christian marriage is the making of the covenant (*foedus*, rather than *contractus*, a contract) between the baptized Christians themselves; it is in virtue of this, and not of any direct ecclesiastical act or intervention, that the new sacramental unity is made by the operation of God in Christ.[6] There were strong pastoral reasons why the disciplinary *Tametsi* decree of the Council of Trent should require the presence of the Roman Catholic priest for the validity of the marriage—they were similar to those which occasioned Lord Hardwicke's Marriage Act in England in the middle of the eighteenth century. But the decree was not intended, and may not be allowed, to distort the Catholic theology of marriage; neither was it designed to be an impediment to the contracting of mixed marriages, of the sort which we are here envisaging, in this era of ecumenical searching which has blessed the later twentieth century. Insistence on its provisions is bound to put the Roman Catholic Church today in an unnecessarily vulnerable position. Theologically considered, it is proper that Christians should come into church for their marriages, in the presence both of their Christian friends and neighbours—the body of Christ, locally animated—and of their priest or bishop, linking this local manifestation of the body with its universality; it is proper that these, too, should communicate together as the body; and, indeed, here—fortunately—is one of the 'proper' things which people ordinarily like to do. But they need not do

[6] See E. Schillebeeckx OP, *Marriage, Secular Reality and Saving Mystery*, Sheed and Ward, London, 1965, 2 vols. G. R. Dunstan, *The Marriage Covenant*, Church Information Office, London, 1961.

it: theologically considered their marriage would be valid if they were free and competent so to marry, and if it were properly contracted according to the laws of their civil society and with the proper dispositions and intent. In our more secularized Western societies there are diminishing social and economic advantages attaching to membership of the Church: people can leave at will. The Church must be on very sure ground, therefore, before it binds upon its people coming to marriage burdens which they can see no compelling reason, in conscience, for them to bear and for which no consistent theological justification can be sustained. It is for this reason that we suggest the danger that the Roman Catholic Church may put itself into an unnecessarily vulnerable position; other Churches may, of course, similarly expose themselves, for other reasons.

One tempting solution to its difficulty would be to allow two priests to minister at a mixed marriage, the one a Roman Catholic, the other an Anglican. This is socially distasteful, theologically a tumour, and to be resisted. It over-clericalizes both the wedding and the ecumenical problem: the over-clericalized wedding ceremony is a true paradigm of our present over-clericalized moves towards union. A true solution must be radical: it must accept, as a minimum, the freedom of the parties to marry in the Church of their choice—guided, no doubt, by the custom of the land—and before the minister of that Church. The recognition by the Second Vatican Council of other Churches as 'means of salvation which derive their efficacy from the very fulness of grace and truth entrusted to the Catholic Church'[7] makes this possible in a way in which it was not before. It opens the way, too, to another step forward—one which many hesitate to take, but which *will* one day be taken when theology liberates us from fear, and puts our minor ecclesiastical differences in perspective: the partaking together in the holy communion at a marriage of Christians communicant in their respective Churches.

The recent statement of the Roman Catholic Ecumenical Commission for England and Wales, entitled *Intercommunion:*

---

[7] Decree on Ecumenism, I, 3.

The Position of the Roman Catholic Church,[8] which referred deferentially to the somewhat fuller treatment of the subject in the Anglican report, *Intercommunion Today*,[9] states the question promisingly, but recoils from it, the promise unfulfilled. Among the indications or occasions for partaking together in eucharistic communion it considers

> the case of a marriage between a Catholic and one who, though not a Catholic, shares much of the Catholic faith including our belief concerning the eucharist: at such a wedding, or at the First Communion of a child of the marriage, the admission of the non-Catholic partner to eucharistic Communion is sometimes suggested (p. 3).
> Our existing unity may also be expressed in connection with the sacraments of marriage and baptism. Catholics may take part as official witnesses (bridesmaid or best man) at the marriages of other Christians, and these may do the same at Catholic marriages . . . (p. 6).

But then the withdrawal begins:

> When it comes to the eucharist . . . Christians of other traditions are welcome to assist, in so far as their conscience allows, as non-communicating members of the congregation to our eucharistic celebrations. *Although it is judged that in present circumstances in England and Wales it will rarely be appropriate*, the possibility is envisaged of Catholics being present as non-communicating members of the congregation at a non-Catholic eucharistic celebration (p. 6, italics ours).

The Episcopal Conference of England and Wales has been discouraging about even this limited participation:

> we must acknowledge that even such attendance at the eucharistic services of our separated brethren will rarely be appropriate as an expression of Christian unity (quoted, *ibid.*, p. 8).

[8] Catholic Truth Society; dated 1968, published 6 March 1969.
[9] Church Information Office, 1968.

It is a privilege which may safely be accorded, generally, to 'mature ecumenists' (p. 9) only, and the context considered is dominantly that of 'ecumenical gatherings'.

This ecclesiastical preoccupation results in communion at a mixed marriage never being considered in the statement. Even in its commentary on n. 55 of the *Directory*, 'Admission to Communion in Special Circumstances', the 'special circumstances' discussed are all the textbook cases of *force majeure,* danger of death, persecution, imprisonment. The whole discussion is dominated by the concepts of 'intercommunion' between divided Churches—by the ecumenical concern, which is primarily an *ecclesiastical* concern: in this preoccupation, the Ecumenical Commission appears to have forgotten the couple entering a mixed marriage, in their spiritual status and need, and at the very point where the essential *unity* of at least two members in Christ is most effectively symbolized.

For this it was rightly criticized in the correspondence columns of the Roman Catholic newspaper, *The Tablet*. The Reverend Charles Crawford, in the issue of 8 March 1969, urged that the mixed marriage was precisely one of the 'special circumstances' which, under the judgment of the diocesan bishop or episcopal conference, would have justified the admission of the non-Roman to communion in the terms of n. 55 of the *Directory*. In this he was supported, on 22 March, by Mr and Mrs John Skinner, Anglican and Roman partners in a mixed marriage. Their letter compacts a theology of the relation of the ecclesiastical sacraments to the sacramental union of marriage, and three paragraphs of it are worth quoting in full:

> It is our conviction that two Christians from separated Churches are privileged frontiersmen in the ecumenical movement: it is their vocation to live out that search for unity to which their Churches are pledged as well as to suffer the disunity that still remains.
>
> It seems to us that by permitting its members to marry separated Christians while withholding the eucharist from the non-Catholic partner (both at the marriage ceremony and

later) Rome contradicts itself. For in a mixed marriage not only do the partners confer the Christian sacrament upon each other (*communicatio in sacris*) but they continue to live out this sacrament for the rest of their lives. Thus, conferring grace upon each other in their daily lives, they are already in communion.

In admitting partners of such a marriage to the eucharist Rome would merely be ratifying an existent sacramental union to which it has already agreed. Such a gesture would become a visible sign of the separated Churches' commitment to unity and, at the local level, a genuine point of contact between two separate parishes

The author of this essay would go a long way with them. He accepts part of the argument for restricting communion in 'ecumenical gatherings' and in all the ecclesiastical peregrinations towards reunion: there is a sense in which, in this context, a sacramental union would be a consummation anticipated, which can be as inappropriate as a prenuptial consummation of marriage. Yet he would not allow this consideration to cast its shadow upon the celebration of a mixed marriage, which must be seen and respected as a union, accomplished in Christ, *in its own right*, to which sacramental communion would give appropriate expression and would confer appropriate grace. He would plead for the liberation of the marriage question from the dominance of ecclesiastical ecumenical diplomacy.

In Holland, in fact, this position has been achieved. A letter from the Roman Catholic Bishops in the Netherlands to all their priests about mixed marriages contained the following paragraph:

When the marriage is celebrated during a celebration of the eucharist and the non-Catholic partner expresses the desire to communicate, we are ready, in conformity with the decree of Vatican II on ecumenism, dated 21 November 1964, no. 8, and with the ecumenical directory for the application of the conciliar decrees on ecumenical affairs dated 14 May 1967, no. 55, to give them this permission on condition that they are baptized, that they can associate themselves with Catholic belief concerning the eucharist, and that in their own Church they are admitted to the Holy Supper.

So much for the making of the marriage. The living of the married life raises questions of a new sort. Hitherto the public discussion has concentrated on the religious upbringing of the children, and the undertakings required by the Roman Catholic Church before it would permit the marriage. A perceptive editorial article in *One in Christ* (1968, no. 2), facing the really difficult case where the mixed marriage is of two convinced and committed Christians of different communions, seeks for a solution which will not violate the proper and well-established Catholic principle that responsibility for the education of children is a *joint* responsibility, one not to be resigned by one parent to the care of the other—a distortion which insistence on the prenuptial undertakings may well provoke. The solution suggested involved the upbringing of the children in *both* Churches, with pastoral provision suitably flexible to encourage the best results from this and to guard against those potentially harmful.

This, then is the proposal which we put forward for the serious consideration of Churches and ecclesial communities which are committed to the ecumenical movement. In such cases children would be jointly baptized; they would join with their parents in family prayers at home, and as they grew older they would be taken to share in the worship of both church-communities, being admitted at the appropriate age to the communion of both Churches. Only when they left the parental home, perhaps to go to university or to get married, would they be obliged to make their own decisions and settle for membership of one Church rather than the other. . . .

It is important to note that what we are proposing here is not a 'lowest common denominator' Christianity which would be acceptable to nobody. Certainly we would propose to build on the basic Christian faith shared by both parents. But an experience of life within the two church-communities is vital to the proposal; the difference between them would have to be explained honestly as and when the child could understand them.

The difficulties attending the proposal are seriously discussed, and the case merits very serious attention in the Churches. It is realistic, in that it takes account of our new cultural situation. It is literally impossible now to rear a child in ecclesiastical isolation—unless he be shut up in an institution firmly closed to the influences of normal school education and the media of radio, television and the press. Services, including the Mass, from the major Christian Churches are broadcast in sound and television; worship in schools, colleges, and many informal societies, is compounded of elements taken from all the great historic traditions; and a new experimenting with informal and *extempore* prayer is—for better or for worse—invading not only those societies but the liturgical life of the Churches themselves. The work of the Joint Liturgical Group, as well as of the major publishing houses, is tending towards the assimilation of liturgical forms, narrowing and even obliterating the differences in worship created by strong traditions in the past. Advantages in this there may be, though too much of it may be regrettable. This, however, is secondary to the main point: that in the atmosphere in which children of mixed marriages are growing up, to educate them in religious, liturgical or ecclesiastical isolation is now impossible; wise pastoral provision will take account of this change, and not base itself on the norms of the ghetto which obtained in the past.

The theological basis of the proposals made in *One in Christ* is the important one of respect for the conjugal unity of the matrimonial couple, and for their joint conscientious decisions. On this basis too, we contend, must be solved the other pastoral disciplines of their respective Churches. The publication of *Humanae Vitae* in July 1968, confirming a discipline established years before, has thus sharpened the problem concerning family planning within the mixed marriage.

The two problems raised by this encyclical for the non-Roman Catholic—the general problem of how a Church formulates its moral judgments and commends them to, or imposes them upon, its members, and the particular problem of how any given couple are to conduct their marriage—were discussed together editorially in *Theology* in February, 1969.[10]. The particular problem is primarily our concern here. Two paragraphs summarize the main considerations in the case:

> *Prima facie*, there can be a head-on collision between one partner restricted by the prohibitions of *Humanae Vitae* and another free to decide for himself the means of discharging the duty of responsible parenthood as declared by the Lambeth Conferences of 1958 and 1968. No doubt there are marriages in which the Anglican can use his liberty by conforming to the Roman restriction; if this is mutually acceptable, happy are they: but such marriages may be few. The critical question remains, whether the Roman partner is in fact similarly free? Can he or she conscientiously practise what the Pope has forbidden? Gregory Baum, in the Introductory essay to Professor Ambrogio Valsecchi's book, *Controversy: The Birth Control Debate 1958-1968*,[11] insists first that the encyclical embodies 'non-infallible' teaching of a sort which has in fact proved erroneous and has been reversed (e.g., in the earlier condemnations of religious liberty, of the critical examination of Holy Scripture, and of Roman Catholic interest in the ecumenical movement). Secondly, he insists that the religious assent owed to such authoritative but 'non-infallible' teaching is conditional, 'i.e., there are conditions under which it is licit for a Catholic to dissent from an official position'. Some episcopal conferences, e.g. the Canadian and the Scandinavian, have asserted the right to dissent. The English and Welsh, like the Belgian, the Austrian and the Dutch, say that 'the primacy of conscience is not in dispute', though without the guidance of the Church 'morality could easily become subjective'; this can only mean that they leave the question of dissent open. The

---

[10] London, SPCK, LXXII, 584. The editor's charitable interpretation of s. 29 of *Humanae Vitae* was criticized by Rev. Paul King in the same journal in April 1969 (LXXII, 586, p. 178).

[11] Geoffrey Chapman, London, 1968. The logic of assent with accommodation is critically examined by Dr James Good in '*Humanae Vitae*, a Platonic Document', *The Tablet*, 19 April 1969.

pastoral task, therefore, is to help the partners in a mixed marriage to decide for themselves whether, for them, conditions for dissent exist.

The Anglican pastor should try first to understand the context in which the Roman Catholic partner forms his mind. Among the documents of Vatican II he should read the Pastoral Constitution, *Gaudium et Spes,* sections 16 on Conscience, 17 on the Excellence of Liberty, 25 on the Interdependence of Person and Society, and 27 on the Reverence for the Human Person: then the critical sections 47 to 52, on Fostering the Nobility of Marriage and the Family. In the Decree on Religious Liberty, *Dignitatis Humanae,* he should read sections 2, 3 and 5, on the duty to act according to conscience and the right not to be forced to act contrary to it, and this in a family context. (*The Documents of Vatican II* is easily available in Walter M. Abbott's edition, published by Geoffrey Chapman in 1966.) He would be wise to read also the addresses of a group of lay Catholics to the Council and to the Magisterium, printed, with other relevant documents, in *On Human Life*.[12] He will then, surely, recall that fundamental theology which is common to both Churches, which sees in marriage a unity where, by the word of the Lord, neither man nor Church may divide. He would serve this unity by encouraging the growth of one conscience, that of the married pair, in place of two potentially in conflict. He would then support the pair in their joint decision as in a *right* decision, not as one ever under the shadow of censure, a sore open to the infection of guilt.

To this, doubtless, words should be added, addressed also to the Roman Catholic pastor, to enable him to inform his mind upon Anglican norms. He may do this from the Report of the Lambeth Conference of 1958,[13] supplemented by the Resolutions of 1968, framed in answer to *Humanae Vitae*.[14] For fuller treat-

---

[12] By Peter Harris *et al.,* Burns and Oates, London, 1968.
[13] SPCK, London, 1958.
[14] *The Lambeth Conference, 1968.* SPCK, London, 1968. The two sets of Resolutions are brought together, though without the supporting argument, in *What the Bishops have said about Marriage,* SPCK, London, 1968.

ment of how the Anglican Communion came to this position he may refer to a study prepared for the Lambeth Conference of 1958, entitled *The Family in Contemporary Society*.[15]

But mere information is not saving grace : the grace which the pastor chiefly needs, whether he be Roman Catholic or non-Roman, is the ability to be of service to the partners of a mixed marriage, and to their family, so that, in ways acceptable to them, he can help them to realize in life the unity that is theirs by marriage. In so doing, they will show to the world something of that unity in Christ, and above all the sheer grace of Christ, which the world so desperately seeks, and to which it may yet again respond when found.

[15] SPCK, London, 1958. Cf. G. R. Dunstan, 'Lawful and Expedient', *The York Quarterly*, May 1960.

7. Growth in Marriage

ROSEMARY HAUGHTON

THE proper thing is for people to marry when they are emotionally mature; they've grown out of childish dependence and learned to stand on their own feet. After that the two of them go ahead with solving the practical problems of married life. They learn to make love enjoyably, cope with illness or financial difficulties, bring up the children, keep on good terms with neighbours and relations, shoulder their responsibilities as citizens and/or Church people. It is quite a programme, in any case, even for these well-balanced, intelligent, generous, hard working (etc., etc., etc.) people that all couples starting married life ought to be.

Maybe there actually are a few couples who correspond to this marriage counsellor's daydream. But I propose to ignore them, for the purposes of this essay, because for one thing I have never met any, so I cannot fairly say anything about them, and for another they are not much help to the likes of us. For most of us differ from them in two essential respects. First of all most couples are nowhere near emotionally mature when they marry. Either or both are likely to be in some degree still dependent and 'ungrown-up'. Many people marry precisely because they long for someone to depend on. It is all wrong according to the books, but it is what often happens and will continue to happen unless some horribly Utopian government introduces a compulsory premarital psychiatric test to prove emotional fitness to wed.

The other respect in which most couples do not fit the notion of the ideal marriage is that even when they are, or soon become, reasonably mature and 'equal' in their relationships they do not stop developing emotionally and spiritually, thank God. People who continue without noticeable change in their outlook, way of life, and emotional responses throughout the course of their married life are people who have stopped growing. And for a human being to stop growing means the same as for a tree to stop growing. It is beginning to die. It may take a long time for its moribund condition to become apparent, but it exists. And when people change they have to get used to their new selves, and that is sometimes as difficult as getting used to being their first, childish self. It means needing support. So a marriage that seemed to have achieved a good, equal relationship and a secure family life may need to re-make itself into something quite different. This can happen several times.

In both these main ways—lack of emotional maturity on marriage, and occasional fairly drastic changes in personality in one or both partners as time goes on—the *majority* of married couples do not conform to the ideal of the advice page of women's magazines, and of the pop-medicine, pop-psychology, pop-theology handbooks on marriage. Yet a surprising number of people remain married, remain sane, and even continue to love each other. But many unfortunately remain married and remain sane, but gradually substitute a mild tolerance and indifference for love. And sometimes even the tolerance is only a façade maintained by a refusal to see a real person under the domestic routine. It seems likely that in many cases this deterioration in the relationship (even when it reaches the point of marital breakdown) is due to the kind of expectation of marriage to which I referred. Both emotional immaturity on marriage, or unexpected developments in emotional reactions and behaviour later on, are looked on as evils, to be ignored or suppressed or compensated.

My suggestion is that they are in fact not only normal and to some extent unavoidable, but are the very condition of spiritual —that is, human—growth in the married state. Perhaps it is not too much to hope that Christians at least, when preparing for marriage or helping others to prepare for marriage, may one day learn to regard it as axiomatic that such emotional 'inadequacies' or 'dangers' are elements in the situation to be accepted in a positive way as opportunities. They are the tests of love and its opportunity for growth. The kind of attitude people have makes all the difference, and this includes the attitude of 'outside' people —relations, advisers, friends.

The easiest way to think about these 'growing points' in marriage is to take a few imaginary examples of a very ordinary kind and see what happens when they are regarded as dangers or 'illnesses' in the marriage, and when they are regarded as challenges in a developing situation.

A young couple get to know each other at a college of education. They fall in love and decide to marry. The girl is from a well-to-do, rather intellectual family in which the parents have both been rather self-consciously liberal in their ideas. Both had careers, both wanted their daughter to have lots of freedom, opportunity, no emotional restraints or parental demands. There has been travel, parties, interesting contacts, and a certain (carefully concealed) disappointment at her decision to become anything so dull as a primary school teacher. The boy comes from a nice, solid, gregarious but unadventurous lower middle-class family. His father has a grocery business; they have always lived in the same pleasant, tidy, well-run semi-detached home with its small but well-stocked and friendly garden. To this girl, this settled, well-ordered, unchanging life is all that she has never had. Warmth, closeness, reliability—she wants these things and 'sees' them in her fiancé. He, on the other hand, sees in her the image of the self-reliant world of successful, adventurous, unconventional people. What to her means safety to him means suffocation. Only neither realizes this.

After they leave college, they marry, and the boy finds that his wife's veneer of blasé self-reliance cracks quickly. She wants to be reassured, told what to do, comforted, helped through every decision; she wants to be praised for minor domestic achievements and cries if he is moody, or comes home late. She has not given up teaching—this would contradict the family image too much—but she finds it a strain, the children upset her easily, she wants to be sympathized with and boosted for the next day's efforts. In fact, she needs a father to lean on, she needs to 'fill in' the missing dependence of childhood. What her husband wanted was a partner who would help him to break out into the wider world of opportunity. So he feels resentful as well as rather helpless, and this makes her more tearful and more desperately clinging. It is a familiar situation, in one form or another. Both feel 'let down' and secretly (or not) blame the other for failing them.

The outcome probably depends on the kind of attitude that 'outside' people take; at the time, or earlier. If either set of parents, for instance, is able to realize the nature of the difficulty they can help to show the husband that although his wife needs, now, to be helped as if she were a little girl, this will not last for ever if he can give her that help. They can help the wife to realize the reason for her own feelings, to appreciate how much she is asking of her husband, and to make an effort to appreciate what he does do and not be frightened by his occasional failures. However enlightenment comes, the decision to tackle the real situation, indeed of continuing to demand a fantasy one and resent its non-existence, will probably lead to a growth in mutual understanding, in real love and generosity on both sides, and in emotional growth for both of them. In time (though the need may recur in times of stress, or may remain, though less obviously) the young wife will grow through the dependent stage and perhaps become able to be the sort of partner her husband hoped for. Or maybe she never will, but he will learn to appreciate her in a different role. In either case there is real growth.

The depressing alternative is often seen—the ambitious husband whose wife is a resented drag, or a background convenience whom he tolerates kindly enough but never treats as an equal. It is true that in many cases people struggle through to a creative solution of such difficulties without actually recognizing, intellectually, what is the matter, but the chances of their doing so are greater if they have some understanding, and above all if their attitude to marriage is open, and prepared for such challenge. The great enemy of growth in marriage is the assumption that 'compatibility', 'fulfilment', and so on, are things one is entitled to as a basis for marriage, rather than things that can come, with effort and patience, as a by-product of continuing growth in love.

It is surprising how many people assume that once one is

'grown-up' in years no more major changes in personality are to be expected. Adolescents may be variable and unexpected, that is understood, but the married couple of, say, ten years are regarded as 'settled'. But it is often just such a period of successful, 'settled' contented married life, with a decent job and several children, that provides the security in love which is needed to release new spiritual potential. It does not have to be spectacular. Sometimes it means that a woman who has been content with home routine and home pleasure feels the need for something more, and finds a 'new' self in some voluntary work or part-time job, or perhaps in being more available to people round about who need her. It may be a man who suddenly finds that his job seems stuffy and confining, and wants to try something quite new, emigrate, go into politics, and so on. In either of these and similar cases, the reaction of the other partner is often one of fear and resentment at the 'upsetting' of the old contented routine. Again, the outcome depends on whether there is a 'security first' attitude, or whether there is an expectation of change and challenge, and a willingness to cope with it. But the onus is not all on the one who wants to 'stay put'; if there is real insecurity in one partner a determination to go ahead at all costs is as destructive of love as the refusal to budge. Openness with each other, a recognition of the nature of each other's needs, can make it possible to work through it together, so that *both* can grow.

One of the most common reasons for radical change in the character of a marriage is probably a disaster of some kind. Loss of job, a serious illness, the death of a child, or the birth of a handicapped child—these are serious and far-reaching events in family life. Unlike the deliberate decision to make a change, they are forced on the couple, but they also require a decision and it is a very similar one. The decision is, basically, whether to 'open out' to the new situation with as much courage and love as possible, or whether to resent it, and 'put up' with it, since it cannot be avoided. An event of this kind also often exposes weaknesses of character that might otherwise have remained unnoticed. At the same time, the challenge can bring out unexpected strengths.

Here is another imaginary example, to make the point clearer.

A farmer in his thirties is married to a woman a year or so younger. They have several children, a reasonable income and a nice home. There have been worries, of course, but the general evenness of life in the country has helped the wife, once a rather neurotic teenager from a possessive family, to find content and security and enjoy her children. The husband becomes ill with polio. He recovers, but is no longer able to walk properly, although he can manage with crutches, and his general health is poor. He can no longer manage the farm, even through an agent, because the strain of decision-making and responsibility is too much in his weakened condition. But he can, after a while, cope with an office job. All this means that the family not only have to move to a town, where he can get work, but they have a much smaller income. The children have to go to big schools, where there is the risk of bullying and the classes are large. They miss their friends and the more relaxed atmosphere of the country. The wife's veneer of placidity wears thin. In a small ugly flat, assailed by the children's complaints, too worried to make friends, she is unable to face the future. She clings to her husband, wanting support, at a time when he himself is deeply depressed and discouraged and humiliated by his 'failure' and guilty about his children's altered lives. Unable to face his wife's demands, he stays out late at the pub and comes home at least slightly drunk. His wife feels even more frightened and desperate. One day she tries to commit suicide by swallowing a bottle of aspirins. She recovers, but the situation is, of course, unchanged, and still has to be lived with. If nothing alters, the end of this is possibly another, successful, suicide attempt, or desertion by the husband, or the dragging on of the misery at a level just above what is totally unbearable. It also means disturbed and delinquent children.

Cases of this type are all too familiar. With a conventional non- or sub-Christian attitude to marriage there is little hope of any real belief in such a situation. Yet the New Testament makes it clear that a loss of self-reliance and confidence in material things is the prerequisite for conversion. If there is even a little willingness left to hope and to love such a marriage can be helped. The realization of each other's fears and weakness and need, the willingness to put this first rather than one's own misery—this is the way through. If the wife can try (with however much interior struggle) to realize why her husband needs the 'break' of the pub companionship, and ceases to reproach him, he may respond by coming home earlier (and sober) and his appreciation of her effort and of her unhappiness would make it easier for him to cope with his own disappointment and humiliation. If each can realize the other's love they can relax a little, make the most of what they have, and find a new experience of love. Even if material conditions do not improve, the growth of compassion between the couple, their concern for each other (even if it fails sometimes) and for their children can change the situation and change the children's future. There can be spiritual growth beyond all expectation, and certainly beyond anything that might have occurred if life had continued prosperous and secure.

This is an extreme case, but all kinds of set-backs that reveal faults and weaknesses are also potential 'growing-points'. Anyone who knows a deeply devoted married couple will probably discover on investigation that their life has passed through some such crisis, often more than one, and they will admit that these were the occasions when they 'really got to know each other', a new life began—often a hard one, but one far more deeply rewarding than in earlier days.

The most common, indeed the inevitable testing time for a marriage comes with middle age, often late middle age, when the children are growing up. Up to a certain point married people generally look ahead, they are always working for something, or towards something—a home of their own, their children's success, getting established in a good job, and so on. But one day, perhaps gradually, it becomes clear that there is no particular goal that *necessarily* commands their energy and hope any more. Whether or not they have achieved what they set out to do, the 'upward' slope of life is over, psychologically if not in fact, and there is a curious blank feeling. People at this stage are not quite sure who they are, or what they are for. They look at the person they have married, perhaps for the first time just as a person, and not as someone with whom they were working, hoping, struggling. This is the time when so many marriages stop growing. People settle down to tolerate each other, look after each other in a dutiful way, or relieve their disappointment and general sense of emptiness with more or less mild nattering and criticism, with time-filling ploys or friends, or sometimes with a bit of adultery, either in fantasy or in fact.

But the very fact that the 'emptiness' of the situation reveals each to the other in a new kind of nakedness is the opportunity for new growth. So much that was only incidentally important has gone, so many needfully cherished illusions can no longer be sustained. Each is exposed to the other in his or her basic human weakness and need, with all the faults, little or great, that are no longer disguised by the need to get on with the job, by beauty, by professional ability, or the busyness of family life. Each, therefore, is a challenge to the other's generosity and love. It is comparatively easy to serve someone you are in love with, or whose qualities you can admire (keeping the others out of sight); it is less easy to appreciate and love the real quality of a person you know very well, and whose weaknesses you cannot disguise any more. (This encounter can, of course, come much earlier and there is an element of it in every crisis in married life, but advancing age is the greatest test.) Yet it is a fact that very many married couples achieve their deepest and most satisfying relationships in later life. Their response to each other—a mixture of admiration, amusement, compassion, tenderness and a sort of obstinate hopefulness—gives them the inner security they need to face the new stage of life, and frees them from selfish worries and self-pity, so that they can often begin a new life in more ways than one. They may travel a bit, or keep open home for grandchildren, and other young people in need of friendship. They may take on all sorts of new work—local voluntary work, study in a new field, or more ambitious pursuits. They clearly enjoy each other, as opposed to simply enjoying doing things together. Both of these things matter, and the second does an enormous amount to make the first possible, but it is the first that counts for most in the long run.

It can be said, then, that there is no event, happy or disastrous, in married life that cannot be an opportunity for growth, for the deepening of love and the freeing of spiritual power. This is only surprising to people who suppose that the teaching of Christ, and the theology which tries to understand it, is a matter entirely separate from the basic needs of ordinary people. The kingdom of heaven is within you and is revealed to the one who searches—'seek and you shall find'. But the search must be made in the hope that comes from trust and love, not out of an arrogant confidence, or a conviction that one has a 'right' to a happy marriage, and that if anything goes wrong and the desired happiness is elusive, it is someone else's fault. The search for the pearl of great price is made at considerable cost: love in marriage grows out of a willingness to lose everything else if necessary. This is not a lesson people usually learn all at once, but if there is even a little real love it grows gradually. It starts small, but it can leaven the whole lump.

But it is also true that 'to him that hath, shall be given'. People who have learned to approach situations with openness and love can face up to tragedies that would crush others. And perhaps this is where it becomes apparent that what decides whether a particular crisis leads to growth or decay is not a matter for the couple only.

Some few people can dredge up from within themselves the courage and endurance and generosity to cope unaided with the most terrible situations. When this is so, it is because in earlier life such people have learned the meaning of love, have been given confidence by the love and example of others. But more often than not the balance tips one way or the other because of the presence or absence of outside help and support at the time. St Paul places marriage 'in the Lord', in the fellowship of God's people, and makes it the expression, mystery, sacrament of this peoples' existence 'in the Lord'. The setting of a marriage in a community where there is or is not someone to understand, to listen, to support, to help in any way, is what makes or mars it. Help may be a matter of doing the washing up and listening to a complaint, or it may mean providing skilled professional help or advancing a deposit for a home. Whatever it is, it only helps if it is part of a general attitude that sees it as *normal* for people to need help. It is not shameful, it is not cause for guilt or despair, it is simply something that needs to be tackled as lovingly as possible. Nothing can make pain, sorrow or anxiety pleasant. Love can turn them into the means of spiritual transformation.

But this attitude that can give practical, loving and continued support to married people is not *outside* them. If it is to work fully it must be part of their own attitude, as I suggested earlier. There are thousands and thousands of marriages that fail to grow, not because of any spiritual rottenness in the couple but because they absorb the wrong attitudes and expectations from their surroundings. This is not a situation we can remedy completely or partly. Most of the energy of people who try to help married couples goes in picking up the pieces after the smash.

All the same, I would like to end this essay on a vastly important subject by suggesting that priests and teachers in general who have some influence over the young, also parents, and the priests who influence *them* in the pulpit and elsewhere, should devote a great deal more thought and time to trying to create the right attitude to marriage. Let us forget about possible sins in marriage, about the need for married people (or at least wives) to be unselfish, holy and patient. They will more easily be these things if they realize from the cradle that the Christian world is one of hope. Christians should look forward, creatively, openly—and always *further*. They are not trying to 'achieve' something here —not even a good marriage. The good marriage *happens* because people have a generous, hopeful attitude to each day's needs and demands. Children who learn this kind of approach to life from parents and teachers and priests are very likely to make good and lasting relationships in marriage. And if, when they are married, they can take for granted the love, sympathy, support and practical help of others with the same attitude, the love in their marriage that begins small (inevitably surrounded by so much selfishness and doubt and fear) will grow like the mustard seed, until all the birds of the air can shelter in its branches.

8. Birth Regulation: Future Prospects

BERNARD PARKER

THE publication of the encyclical *Humanae Vitae* in July 1968 was followed by statements by the hierarchies of many countries seeking to interpret the Pope's words and to help the laity to apply them. Discussion of the encyclical and its implications will continue for some while to come: it is therefore an appropriate time to review our knowledge of birth regulation by the use of the infertile phases of the menstrual cycle ('safe period' or the 'rhythm method') and to try to foresee in which directions progress may be made consistent with the ideals of responsible parenthood to be found in the encyclical.

THE RHYTHM METHOD

The assessment of any method of family planning can properly be undertaken under four headings—applicability, acceptability, safety and efficiency.

Applicability.

The question at issue here is whether a given method of birth control is practicable in different circumstances. Limiting factors include expense, the need for regular medical supervision, and the availability of the drug or device. The rhythm method cannot be faulted in respect of any of those factors. It requires initially, careful instruction by an informed person or persons but thereafter very little expense or trouble is involved. There must be a motivation towards success, however. Some degree of intelligence is necessary but work among the under-privileged (e.g. in Mauritius) has shown that no high level of education is required to enable a couple to chart the basal body temperature daily and to interpret the chart.

Considering the body of knowledge now available, it is regrettable that nowhere, so far as I know, have modern mass-media been used to instruct in the method. The opportunity to teach by television is one which Catholic countries might have been expected to seize. It is, of course, clear from experience in Britain that this would not be enough by itself. The basic facts have to be leavened with an understanding of the place of sex in marriage and no TV lesson can take the place of the individual counselling service which allows a couple to interpret the facts in the light of their personal needs. But instruction by TV or film or radio could sow the seed, could help to present the facts and could supplement the personal interview. For nations or communities with a population problem and the necessary facilities, the lesson seems obvious. Until such an approach is tried the applicability of the method to 'people' as opposed to some privileged persons within a population cannot be said to have been put to the test.

Acceptability

Ethical considerations will be dominant in decisions concerning the acceptability of this method but I shall concern myself chiefly with certain medical matters.

If the rhythm method is to achieve success, it must be built into the foundations of the marriage. It is fruitless to expect a couple who have grown accustomed to undertaking sexual intercourse with no thought of restraint to alter this pattern after years of marriage without real hardship and the possibility of trauma: hence the importance which has been attached to courses on preparation for marriage by the Catholic Marriage Advisory Council. When marital love coexists with prudence from its beginning, the method can be, and for many is, wholly acceptable.

Nevertheless particular difficulties are encountered which ought not to be ignored in certain groups and at certain times. The problem of a woman with an irregular menstrual cycle can be resolved by the use of hormones, so-called regulators, which are in many cases identical with the contraceptive pill (hereinafter called the 'pill'). When control of the periods is taken over in this way, fertility may also be excluded for a time, but in such cases the treatment is stopped at intervals and will not be recommenced if normal rhythm has been restored.

A similar, if temporary, difficulty occurs after childbirth and a recent study by Cronin shows the pattern of return to fertility in such cases.[1] With this knowledge, married couples can return to a life in which birth control is re-established with the help of the temperature chart. Yet for some, especially those who have had to refrain from intercourse in the latter part of pregnancy, a further interval of abstinence before resuming coitus will be hard to bear. The use of the pill has been advocated at this time to ensure the natural infertility of the post-partum phase. Since Cronin has shown that the natural infertile phase following birth is variable but may be quite brief, it is difficult in my view to see this use of the pill as other than contraceptive in intent.

Another time of difficulty comes before the menopause and this affects not a minority but the majority of marriages and in some may last for years rather than months or weeks. During this time, ovulation occurs erratically and though fertility is low, its absence cannot be guaranteed. Workers in the field of family planning have lately been satisfied that the pill is effective and acceptable at this time and its use may well be justified for Catholics in the presence of an irregular cycle. It is unfortunate that its slight but definite medical risk is enhanced in this age group.

In discussing these difficulties, we clearly require to know the facts concerning sexual activity at such times. Kinsey[2] in his well-

---

[1] T. J. Cronin, 'Influence of lactation upon ovulation', *The Lancet*, 24 Aug. 1968, p. 422.
[2] A. C. Kinsey, *Sexual behaviour in the human female*, Saunders, Philadelphia and London, 1953 (also Foursquare paperback, 1966).

known report did not refer to coitus during and after pregnancy but the recent report on *Human Sexual Response* by Masters and Johnson states that for some couples, strong sexual interests returned in the woman within two or three weeks of childbirth and among women who were breast-feeding there was a prompter-than-average return.[3] In Kinsey's sample of menopausal and post-menopausal women there is clear evidence that, for some at least, sexual responses and activities are not diminished at this time.

It is possible to postulate that at times of difficulty a woman's libido (and a man's also) may be decreased (e.g. because after childbirth, her attention is concentrated on the baby). If true, this would be convenient for her family planning advisers. It is, however, equally reasonable to argue that at times of stress, a woman may welcome and even rely upon demonstrations of marital love to sustain her and to maintain the unity of the family. Christian writers, seeking to understand and to help, may with reason suspect that some evidence such as that which is quoted above is biased by materialism in our society and does not truly reflect the situation among Christian couples. There is no reason, however, to deny the existence of such difficulties, whatever their gravity or frequency, and the answer to the objections must surely lie in further research into sexuality among Christian married men and women.

Another objection to periodic continence is based on the claim that a woman may be most inclined to respond to love-making at mid-cycle, at the very time when she has, perforce, to exercise restraint. The evidence quoted by Kinsey does not support this belief, for only ten per cent of women in his series claimed maximum sensitivity at this time. Since this group had access in most cases to contraception (only 12 per cent were Catholics), his result is unlikely to have been influenced by the psychological 'pull' of a time when intercourse has the attraction of 'forbidden fruit'. Once again, further research among couples practising the rhythm method would help to settle the size of this problem.

[3] W. H. Masters and V. E. Johnson, *Human sexual response*, Boston, Little, Brown and Co., 1966.

The difficult case—Summary

What seems clear is that there are some couples for whom the denial of intercourse at times of difficulty represents a serious threat to the sexual component of their marriages, and for them periodic continence may be little easier to accept than a total ban on intercourse. Marshall[4] issued a questionnaire concerning the psychological effects of abstinence on the couples participating in his birth regulation study.[5] Although two-thirds found the method generally satisfactory, a quarter of the couples believed it had had a harmful effect on their relationship. (It would be interesting to know what the answer would be from couples who used this method from the start of the marriage.) In some but not all situations of difficulty, the use of the pill is morally acceptable. When abnormal menstrual conditions are present it can be used to treat this irregularity in the body of one marriage partner and thereby confer benefit on the marriage itself. But it cannot be used to correct 'marital pathology' in the absence of this bodily disease. This is the present situation which will continue to be discussed and which presumably elicited the exhortation to persevere in the section of *Humanae Vitae* which referred compassionately to the 'serious difficulties inherent in married life'.

Safety

Infertile phase advice has, in this respect, an edge over all other methods of birth control, being entirely free from physical ill-effects. The safety of a method is, however, closely bound up with its efficiency since a less efficient method (even if an inherently safer one) will permit more unplanned pregnancies and each pregnancy can bring risk to the mother.

As a simple (if perhaps, *too*-simple) illustration, let us imagine one million women using two family planning methods for one

[4] J. Marshall, 'Psychological aspects of the basal-body-temperature method of regulating births', *Fertility and Sterility* (in the press).

[5] J. Marshall, 'A field trial of the basal-body-temperature method of regulating births', *The Lancet,* 6 July, 1968, p.8.

year each. Using the contraceptive pill with its very low failure-rate, a total of one thousand (to, at the most, ten thousand) unplanned pregnancies would occur. With the present maternal death-rate of 0.2 to 0.3 per thousand pregnancies no more than one or two women out of the original million would be likely to die as a result of childbirth. But, on the evidence of recent reports, thirty women might expect to die in the year from thromboembolism, making a total mortality of 31 associated with the pill.

If one million women were using the rhythm method, none would die from any condition directly attributable to the method. But, with the use of Marshall's figures[6], sixty-six thousand women would be pregnant (if coitus were restricted to the post-ovulatory phase) and one hundred and ninety-three thousand would be pregnant if intercourse occurred both before and after ovulation. Fifteen to twenty women from the first group and forty to sixty from the second might be expected to die as a result of their pregnancy.

Obviously these calculations are so facile as to be worthless as an estimate of the *value* of a method but they illustrate how the safety of a method cannot be assessed in isolation from its efficiency. Nor is mortality the only criterion of safety, though it is the most dramatic. Morbidity (or damage short of death) must also be taken into consideration. The only valid criticism of the safe period method on this score is the psychological trauma which it may cause in those couples who cannot accept the restrictions involved. By comparison, there are very real hazards to health associated with modern birth control methods, such as the intra-uterine device and the pill. All in all, in the matter of safety the rhythm method is unsurpassed. More will be said on this very important aspect later.

Efficiency

A recent trial of the efficiency of the temperature method of birth regulation was carried out by clients of the Catholic Marriage

[6] *op. cit.*

Advisory Council and reported by Marshall in *The Lancet*.[7] Where intercourse took place before and after the fertile phase each month, the failure rate was 19.3 pregnancies per 100 woman-years. When intercourse occurred only after evidence of ovulation was seen on the temperature chart the failure rate was 6.6. These figures have to be set against a rate of less than 1.0 for the pill, and less than 5.0 for the intra-uterine device. To achieve the better figure (6.6), intercourse has to be restricted to approximately one week in four and abstinence of this order must be difficult in practice for many couples. The higher figure (19.3) is wholly unsatisfactory if the indication to avoid pregnancy is a serious one. It is possible that these figures could be reduced without altering the method since they show user-effectiveness and the efficiency of the method, perfectly applied (the biological effectiveness), is very much greater. But it is also true to say that the couples concerned in this trial must count as well-motivated and it seems probable that in most communities a similar failure-rate would apply in practice! Another study from the United States at about the same time gave a comparable result (19.5 per 100 woman-years).[8]

Comment on the method

It would be a mistake to dismiss the rhythm method simply because of its high failure-rate, for certain other relevant facts alter the picture considerably. The relatively high percentage of failures is apt to obscure the large number of couples for whom the method has been a complete success. For them, birth regulation has in fact been achieved by a means which involved them in no physical risks, no therapeutic side-effects, no unaesthetic interference in the act of intercourse (and minimal expense and trouble). I am not concerned here to put the much more important positive aspects of the notion of responsible parenthood which, by underwriting the method, give it its special merit in

---

[7] *op. cit.*
[8] Bartzen, P. J. 'Effectiveness of the temperature rhythm system of contraception'. *Fertil. Steril.* (1967) 18.694.

present-day marriage practice. I merely note that, whenever the method is found acceptable by a married couple, having been put into practice from the beginning of marriage, it will often remain their method of choice without consideration of any other. Even if an unplanned pregnancy occurs, the end-result for an average healthy couple is likely to be well within the limits of acceptability. Given this background I believe that infertile phase advice cannot be bettered as a first choice in Christian marriage. It would, however, be wrong to gloss over its weakness, viz. its liability to failure, and for those with serious reasons to avoid pregnancy (e.g. on medical grounds) the published figures do nothing to allay anxiety.

THE FUTURE

Because of this anxiety, men of science have been encouraged by the Pope 'to explain more thoroughly the various conditions favouring a proper regulation of births' and to provide 'a sufficiently secure basis for a regulation of births founded on the observance of natural rhythms'. Two possibilities can be envisaged in this regard.

The first is a more perfect indicator of the exact time of fertility. It should be realized that there are already at least a dozen scientific methods of ascertaining the fertile phase of the cycle, of which the shift in basal temperature (together with the recognition of ovulation pain and an ovulatory discharge of mucus) remains the most efficient means available to persons in the ordinary setting of their homes. As yet, no practicable method detects *impending* ovulation; all methods spot the event or conditions following the event. It is certainly possible that some means of recognizing the ripe follicle (a day or two ahead of the release of the ovum) may be found, but it is pertinent to observe that a 24 hour 'warning' would be too late to prevent conception and it is difficult to foresee the development of what is really required, an alarm set accurately for 3 or 4 days before the event.

If it is difficult to envisage the development of a perfect indicator, is there greater hope of controlling the time of ovulation? This idea of a 'pill' for Catholics, one which would not prevent ovulation but which would control its timing, has been taken up with some enthusiasm and before discussing the prospects it is important to note that real hazards, ethical and physical, are implicit in the notion of a pill to 'regularize' the fertile time.

Let us consider first the use of a pill which would 'trigger' the release of the ovum at a known time. Such a substance might be seen as assisting a natural process rather than frustrating it and might be acceptable to moralists. It is very doubtful however whether any precision could be achieved in practice by the use of this hypothetical 'starter-gun' hormone. The alternative is to aim at delaying the release of the ripening ovum by medication until a given day when, on release of the inhibition (by stopping the drug), ovulation would follow and therefore be predictable. The analogy here is the box-start (instead of the starter's gun) in which the early arrivals are made to wait for the late. This latter method is more open to the charge of interference with a natural pattern and might not be acceptable to the moral theologian. However, it is the medical, not the ethical, snags to which I am concerned to draw attention here and in this regard we can turn with profit to experience built up as a result of the widespread use of the contraceptive pill.

Hazards of the contraceptive pill

It is not my intention to be alarmist about the pill. In its role as a contraceptive it has proved efficient beyond all expectation and it has been screened and studied as thoroughly as any therapeutic substance in medical history. Furthermore, *when regarded as a therapeutic substance* it can properly be classified as 'safe'. Why then does it continue to be the source of so much discussion and some anxiety?

The facts are these. There is an acknowledged risk in a minority of cases of provoking thrombosis, notably in the lower limbs and pelvis but possibly also within the brain and, it has been suggested recently, in the liver veins. The risk of a woman being admitted to hospital because of leg vein thrombosis is increased by five to ten times by the use of the pill. Out of every one hundred thousand women on the pill, it is thought that two or three die annually due to its use. Other risks, less serious but disquieting, include a tendency towards the diabetic state, headache, possibly of vascular origin and loss of libido. Of course drug effects are not all adverse and beneficial effects of the pill include relief of painful periods, reduced menstrual bleeding and possibly some protection against cancer of the body of the uterus.

No powerful substance used in the treatment of disease is entirely safe (not even penicillin, certainly not aspirin). When it is used to treat bodily disease the pill can be described as one of the safer therapeutic agents. However, when used as a contraceptive, different standards must apply. If a woman's life or health is at risk from pregnancy, then the slight risk of the pill is clearly justified, as it is in the treatment of gynaecological disease. However, for many women using the pill, the indications are socio-economic only, and other contraceptive methods could be used (even if less efficient ones). In this situation, the prescription of a drug with even a slight risk must be weighed by the doctor on a different scale of values. This is a crucial point and the question is put in a recent *British Medical Journal* leader,. 'Should a doctor give a *healthy* young woman a prescription for an oral contraceptive if it may lead to her death?' (my italics). In addition doctors are properly concerned about possible long-term adverse effects when, as here, large numbers of healthy women are involved and an alternative is available. In this scale of values, the fact that no long-term effects have as yet been seen fails to provide total reassurance.

For this reason, I am alarmed by the idea of using any substance simply to achieve greater predictability of ovulating. Such therapeutic agents are bound to have their side-effects and their snags, if not their dangers. In this particular instance, there is the additional hazard of causing genetic damage, when the target-organ is the ripening follicle in the ovary. Substances which stimulate ovulation are already in use among infertile women. In such cases it is reasonable, with the patient's consent, to explore the potentialities of drugs such as clomiphene. It would be a very different matter to propose to use a drug of this kind on a wide basis in *healthy* women. Even when the short-term effects had been assessed, the worry of long-term sequelae and the effect on any child conceived whilst on therapy—both on the child itself and on its genetic inheritance—makes me reluctant to consider, still less to recommend, any scheme for 'precision ovulating' by the use of a pill.

This somewhat gloomy view of the prospects for efficient contraception within the bounds of the present norms of the Church is a purely personal one. It certainly does not imply that there should be any lack of encouragement of research work in this field—rather the reverse—and, as in other spheres, new light may appear tomorrow where hopes seem dim today. With these thoughts in mind I turn to consider planning for the future.

PLANNING FOR THE SEVENTIES

It is clearly desirable when choosing a method of birth regulation that it should be efficient. Yet I believe it worth examining further the question 'Do we really want *total* control of fertility?' At present, absolute or near-absolute control comes only from total continence on the one hand or the pill and certain sterilizing procedures on the other. (There is a *biological* failure-rate in the rhythm method of over 1 per hundred woman-years.) No person can approve a feckless approach to parenthood or the needless procreation of an 'unwanted' child. Yet in the modern planned family it seems there may be no room for error, no place for the unexpected pregnancy. This mechanistic view of the number of children—no more than and perhaps no less—is so far removed from the human condition of which we are clearly not the supreme masters that it should be condemned as unreal and unchristian, and noted to have inherent dangers. . . . 'The best laid schemes o' mice and men gang aft agley', Burns noted, and few families in their history fail to bear this out.

One result of the expectation of certainty in birth control is the tendency for patients to return to their doctor, in the event of an unplanned pregnancy, asking for abortion. In the new climate following the Abortion Act 1968, it is implied that the prescribing doctor is responsible for the failure and ought to make good *his* mistake. Not many doctors will accept this reasoning, but if, from their respect for new life, they manage to dissuade the woman, some would be prepared to offer sterilization after delivery, since contraceptive measures have already failed. This illustrates the thesis, widely held in the West, that respect for life itself should be much nearer to the absolute than respect for the life-giving faculties: in other words, abortion is a much greater evil than contraception. Whilst this thesis remains unchallenged, it should be noted that in practise the gap between the two has narrowed and in certain cases the border-line is now somewhat blurred.

Difficulty for the theologian comes from the doctor's uncertainty as to the mode of action of some of the new 'pills'. The original pill blocked ovulation and was therefore a temporary sterilizing agent. The newer pills, different in composition and lower in dosage, do not always inhibit ovulation. They may prevent conception by altering the mucus of the neck of the womb in which case they act as 'barrier' contraceptives. If, however, they achieve their effect by neither of these means, but by creating a hostile lining of the womb which prevents the embedding of the fertilized egg, they become a kind of abortifacient (as is the intrauterine device—I.U.C.D.—in all probability).

At present, most of my non-Catholic colleagues tend to disregard these theoretical considerations, taking refuge in the clear distinction of *intention*, evident when one compares the action of a man who attempts to prevent pregnancy with the frankly destructive activity of one who procures an abortion. It is probable that the development of a 'morning-after pill' (which would of course be abortifacient) would not arouse much conscientious objection amongst doctors. But the need to distinguish carefully will become apparent at the next stage in development when (and if) a pill is produced which would attack and kill the embryo which is beginning to grow in the womb: when, in other words, a pill is available which will procure abortion.

Developments such as these have not made the lot of the theologian any easier; it is for example important to know what moral distinction, if any, can be made between an act which prevents embedding and an act which attacks the embedded conceptus. Progress has not always smoothed the path of the doctor either, though it has greatly increased efficiency in fertility control. Many Catholics are convinced that, were it not for the norms of the Church, family planning would be certain, easy and trouble-free. I hope enough has been said to rebut this. Contraceptive measures give two advantages only, higher efficiency (the pill, I.U.C.D., sterilization) and the option of spontaneity in intercourse, but they buy these benefits at a cost. The continued search for alternatives (the male pill, the morning-after pill, contraception by injection, male sterilization) gives proof that no one method of birth control offers a satisfactory solution to all difficulties.

With this background in mind, I would suggest that fully responsible parenthood should rest on the foundation of a programme of education for marriage, which begins in the home, and is continued in schools, and in clubs, and in churches, ending with a preparation for the sacrament of matrimony, commensurate with the grandeur of the task ahead. In this programme, the doctor will have a part to play, only a part, but an important part. It cannot be assumed that people will flock to use such facilities without a formidable effort of persuasion and sales-talk. Modern aids are needed, time and money must be found.

In ideal marriage, the rhythm method properly understood and improved by further researches will provide an ideal means of developing the sexual relationship and of planning the family. Meanwhile the search to improve the efficiency of the method must go on and the support, financial and otherwise, given to research will be some criterion of the response of the people of God to the Pope's message.

All marriages are not ideal marriages, however. A commentator on the pastoral advice offered by various hierarchies following *Humanae Vitae* writes:

> The hierarchies seem to accept that avoidance of contraception is an ideal for the Christian, an ideal which he is expected to achieve and that only serious reasons—especially a conflict of duties—can absolve him from sin, if he fails to achieve it here and now.[9]

It is clearly not expected that all will achieve it here and now, and during the interim those in difficulty are to be helped and kept from despair: they are to be encouraged to use the sacraments. If the priest is not to abandon them, neither surely is their marriage counsellor. What then of their doctor? It behoves him to know not only what is ideal but what, in less perfect circumstances, seems best for these couples. He must be sympathetic and knowledgeable. He must maintain respect for the primacy of his patients' consciences (for any decision is theirs in the end) and then, in accordance with his own conscience, his advice should be given. It seems to cause scandal, at times, that medical advice is not uniform in these cases, that there is no longer in practice a certain, orthodox line. In the light of present difficulties and uncertainties, it would perhaps be more scandalous if *seeming* agreement prevailed when there can as yet be none. It is towards this end, however, that we steer. Further knowledge, technical and theological, will, under God, provide the motive power.

[9] Austin Flannery, O.P., *Doctrine and Life*, 19 (Feb. 1969), p. 106.

9. Marital Problems: A Strategy for Service and Research

DOUGLAS WOODHOUSE

DISCUSSION of the complex and sometimes controversial issues involved can only be brief in a single chapter. But the reader will, I hope, be stimulated to seek out the original sources which provide the background to what follows. It is intended as a contribution to the debate which must precede the development of a total community service, preventive as well as remedial, focused on the marital relationship.

Consideration of such a service must include (i) the social and mental health aspects of marriage and divorce; (ii) the impact of social change, and (iii) the requirements of professional training, practice and cooperation.

First, about the nature of psychological stress in marriage. Conflict and tension are inevitable conditions of living; they are inherent in close personal relationships, especially the intimate relationship of marriage. The experience of these feelings and the attendant anxiety, with their mainspring in the conflictful inner world of each of us, may be so threatening as to immobilize us or lead to an excessive reliance on unconscious defences or 'psychological manoeuvres' aimed at avoidance. Yet the potential for growth and creativity also lies in conflict and tension; without them life and liveliness are limited for the individuals and their relationship.

Intensive work with marriages in trouble has shown that there are very powerful forces leading people towards the maintenance of their marriage. On the other hand, these cohesive forces are frequently threatened by disruptive conflicts to which, at first sight, breaking up the relationship may seem the only solution but which, with more careful consideration and understanding, can often be contained within and even enrich the relationship. Without adequate help premature decisions are often taken, of which children may be the first casualties. Marriage, a heterosexual relationship between two adults, is in itself a dynamic system in which the most powerful feelings, and the stress which may accompany them, can be expressed and contained. Experience suggests that the concept of the containment of stress—stress which continues to be alive and active as change, growth and maturation is experienced—holds good even for very disturbed couples (2, 3, 5, 14, 17, 22).[1] Thus stress in marriage involves mental health issues in a positive as well as a pathological sense.

A frequent outcome of excessive reliance on unconscious defences aimed at keeping conflict out of the relationship is that stress in marriage often shows itself indirectly rather than overtly, particularly in the first instance. This means that a wide range of symptoms, social, emotional and physical, in one or other partner or in their children, are commonly related to the kind and quality of the relationship between husband and wife.

This is because psycho-social disorders, and the relationship problems to which they give rise, usually manifest themselves in specific areas of disfunction; help is usually sought according to the nature of the trouble in this specific area. The marital relationship, even when it is not itself the specific area of trouble, can prove an effective focus for work on many individual and family problems; without this focus many such symptoms prove recalcitrant (6, 7, 13, 22). It follows, therefore, that services offering help with overt marriage problems must be considered in the context of community social services as a whole.

It also follows that understanding and skill in recognizing the psychodynamic functioning of the family group and the uncon-

---

[1] Arabic numerals in parentheses refer to the list of reference works at the end of this chapter.

scious as well as conscious processes involved in marital stress is relevant to all the 'helping professions'. So is their ability to offer help in the light of this—help which is appropriate to those who seek it *and* to the setting in which it is offered, since people choose many different doors on which to knock (6, 8, 22).

This in turn leads to the view that if a strategy for community services is to take account of what is known about the phenomena of marital problems and marital interaction it will involve transcending established boundaries between the traditional academic and professional disciplines—medicine, sociology, law, social work—just as it will need to comprehend a 'mix' of services—those made available under statutory and voluntary, secular and religious auspices, by a range of workers both specialized and non-specialized so far as marital work is concerned. A total community service requires a functional relationship between all these groups. There must be a confrontation of the problems, institutional and technical, which this involves (12, 16).

We know, however, that the psycho-social disorders are usually difficult and slow of resolution, even given access to relationship problems, adequate skill and an appropriate focus. Resistance to change is the rule. We have, therefore, to be suspicious of shortcut techniques which support or encourage false solutions, i.e. methods which aim at adaptation through the avoidance of that level of anxiety which is a requisite for growth and change. Breaking up the relationship is often such a 'false' solution—but not always. A comprehensive approach would provide services for those whose relationship fails. Such a failure involves emotional problems akin to bereavement and both parties may need help in order to work through them, both for their own well-being and that of their children (9).

When a marriage fails or reaches a crisis, it is inevitably due to a complex combination of personality interaction and pressures from the environment which combined in such a way as to exceed the joint resources of the partners. Pressures which split or immobilize one couple may unite and strengthen the relationship between another. Understanding the interaction of the 'inner' with the 'outer' world is crucial. All share the impact of contemporary living, but society exerts different influences as between one social group and another. In this context the environment must also be taken to include that which the family creates within and for itself as a group as well as the pressures and hazards inseparable from the natural life cycle of the family (i.e. the birth of the first baby; the death of the partners' parents; the adolescence and departure of children as they develop their adult sexuality; the menopause). These phases of change often create a time of crisis in a family when preventive intervention with a marital focus may be both acceptable and decisive (8).

General research strategy may conveniently be considered at this point. In order to undertake productive research in our field, as in other areas of human relations, those so engaged need not only training in the behavioural sciences, but also to be participants in professional services. Only in this way are they able to gain access to much of the essential data since human beings are often unwilling, indeed are unable, to reveal their pain, their problems or their motives except in the context of a trusted relationship through which they can be assured of help. Moreover, given that research and service are linked, as they need to be, it is then possible to observe human relations in course of change and so identify, for systematic study, problems of practical significance and the formulation of relevant hypotheses (23).

At the same time as the need emerges for a pattern of services and research that reflect a comprehensive approach which plainly asserts the criteria for choices and decisions, a further set of factors confronts us. These have to do with social change and the increasing pace with which it now takes place. This is likely to affect demand for services qualitatively as well as quantitatively.

A relevant aspect of social change is reflected by the Divorce Reform Bill (which seems certain to become law in much the form proposed). It indicates change in favour of an increase in self-determination and personal responsibility, for hitherto major decisions involving grave moral conflicts for the individual have been taken within a framework of collective responsibility expressed by the Church[2] or the Law[3] (25). This is, in my view, a progressive measure, but it does not remove, and it may in fact sharpen, issues of innocence and guilt because the individual will now have the burden of making such decisions to the best of his or her own ability. Many are likely to feel the need for help with such a task. Experience shows that failure to get help when this need arises can lead to unnecessary divorce, or chronic unhappiness, or both (9).

The Bill also lays explicit stress on reconciliation, a further indication of change. This in a social climate which, in any case, encourages couples to seek help with problems in marriage. There is no doubt that large additional resources as well as a more effective deployment of those that already exist for work with marital problems will be required.

But as the new legislation makes its way to the statute book, a number of conflicting social facts are obvious in the total field. For example, there is an effective disregard for marriage at some levels by those who repeatedly divorce and, as a social institution, it is repudiated by those who pose the question 'Why marry'? Contradictions of this sort in a pluralistic society such as ours, in conditions of rapid overall change, can be expected as can marked differences in the rate of change as between one segment or group in society and another. These contradictions and dissonances increase tension and tend to increase what has been called 'relevant uncertainty', for individuals, for groups, including the family, and for society as a whole. They also tend to make it difficult to be aware of the difference between what is *actually* taking place and what is *supposed* to be taking place. The measures to be taken must therefore not only be comprehensive, they must be flexible and capable of anticipating rather than merely responding to events (19).

---

[2] That this is true not only of the Established Church is suggested by the current debate on contraception and the dogma governing sexual relationships within the Catholic Church.

[3] The Bill itself is part of an accelerating process of change which may be said to have begun more than a century ago when the Matrimonial Causes Act of 1857 transferred matrimonial jurisdiction from the ecclesiastical to the secular courts (25).

It is against this background and in this situation that an array of services has to be mobilized. Experience suggests that it would need to include the following :

(i) *Community services.* (Including for example those provided by the local authority personal social services, those based on hospitals by medical social workers, by psychiatrists and psychiatric social workers, by caseworkers in voluntary agencies, by probation officers. It would of course also include the work of allied professionals, i.e. general practitioners, the clergy.)

(ii) *Specialized marital services.* (Including the probation service in its statutorily defined 'reconciliation' role.)

(iii) *Centres of advanced study and practice.*

The community services

At times of crisis, when problems tend to be sharply defined, the immediately available worker in the field, to whom a specific problem is brought, tends to be the most acceptable source of help, and in crisis established defences are usually disturbed so that this is a propitious time to engender change in the individual and in his relationships. The worker in the 'agency of first instance' frequently has the chance to establish a relationship because he is acceptable, and an opportunity for effective action because of contact in a crisis. If help offered at this point can be insightful enough and can be focused through understanding which throws light on presenting symptoms, a first set of economies can be achieved.

A second set of economies can arise if, through appropriate action, ultimate referral to a 'specialist in marital treatment' is avoided. Referral to another agency is often a necessary and proper development, but it can also be very desirable to offer continuing help in the 'agency of first instance'. This is especially so when a relationship of trust has been established *before* the underlying problem becomes explicit. Referral at the point at which problems in a marriage are exposed often proves abortive because it is construed as a rejection by those to whom the clients have revealed themselves. Referral, when referral is in fact appropriate, must be most carefully carried out if it is to contribute to, rather than hinder, positive change. The need for those in community services is therefore for a level of skill which will enable them to exploit their crucial position without turning aside from their established role. Such work does not involve 'marital casework' in the strict sense, even though workers in these services will always have to continue with, as well as refer, some overt marital problems. But in the main their task is to deal with presenting difficulties in the light of the underlying forces at work, especially those in the relationship between husband and wife. Such an approach demands more skill than is often at present available. It also requires agencies in the field to facilitate practice which can utilize the marital relationship as a focus for its work (6).

The specialized marital services

An increasing number of couples explicitly seek help with marital problems from specialized agencies, professional and non-professional. As noted above, this trend is likely to be accelerated in the future. Increasingly, too, psychiatric centres are perceived as appropriate sources of help by couples themselves and by those who refer, both medical and non-medical workers.

The emotional disturbances underlying the problems brought to workers in these agencies, as to those in the community services, comprise a wide range of complexity and severity with regard to their underlying causes and the sort of psychotherapeutic relationship their treatment requires. The necessary level of skill is therefore not uniform; some couples require more intensive work than others. Good diagnosis is thus essential and there has to be flexibility in technique within and between agencies if the best possible match is to be made between need and available resources. Meanwhile, because some couples feel 'comfortable' and can settle in to work on their problems in one setting and some in another, it is appropriate that a diversity of agencies should be maintained. Experience also shows that it is not only those who seek help who have to be considered; workers also need a facilitating environment because of the special characteristics of intense, ongoing work with marital problems and the particular anxieties these commonly arouse.

The matching of available resources to the increasing demands made upon them is an exceptionally difficult problem. Our diagnostic and therapeutic skills are seldom adequate to meet the complexities of the phenomena confronting us. The pressing need, irrespective of the level of skill required within any one of the different specialized agencies, is that the general level of technical competence should be increasingly developed—the situation requires more than an increase in the *volume* of resources.

Centres of advanced study and practice

If the many different agencies involved are to exploit their strategic positions on the continuum of services, the important issue is the extent to which these groups can increase their contribution in quality as well as quantity. As in the wider area of community mental health within which marital problems are known to play so prominent a part, there is therefore a need for centres of advanced study and practice.

The aim of such centres would be to support those in the field, by furthering the development of professional skills appropriate to the settings in which they are to be practised. As in the first two areas, there are formidable problems to be overcome. A list of the minimum requirements to be met by such centres implies their nature and extent:

(i) The staff must continuously engage in clinical practice if effective training and consultation is to be offered to those in the field, or meaningful and relevant research undertaken.

(ii) Therefore, though it will necessarily have to be small by comparison with the community and specialized agencies, the caseload with which the staff are directly and, through consultation, indirectly involved, should reflect the full range which is met in other settings.

(iii) On the basis of this practice a centre must attempt to develop techniques which, though not necessarily directly transferable, can advance understanding relevant to the field as a whole. Those working in the centre must not be perceived by colleagues in other settings as doing something different and unrelated to their problems.

(iv) The staff of the centre must keep ahead in its thinking and practice so as to provide the expertise needed by colleagues in other agencies.

(v) A centre must embody skills in addition to those of effective treatment, i.e. in consultation and teaching, and it must be able to employ skills in inter- and intra-group relations so as to be able to help with institutional problems of innovation and change which are often highlighted by staff development.

(vi) The behaviour of the staff of the centre must reflect the view that responsibility for what he undertakes rests with the worker concerned; consultation or training must not represent 'taking over' responsibility. This would not only be impracticable and defeat the centre's aims; it is the antithesis of sound inter-professional relationship.

(vii) A centre must, in its own structure and organization, demonstrate a model which contains rather than denies or dissipates the anxiety inseparable from the stress of learning about, and working intensively with, marital problems (11).

These are difficult criteria to meet and maintain, and still more to reproduce in a number of centres in different areas. Yet such 'specialist' centres seem essential to a comprehensive and integrated service (8, 18).

The strategy outlined suggests itself from experience gained by the Institute of Marital Studies (formerly the Family Discussion Bureau) over the past twenty years. Research and development are, however, inseparable and a range of projects is urgently needed. They can be considered under a number of heads and might include the following:

(a) *Epidemiological studies,* which would involve social anthropology and social psychology (4, 15).

(i) To identify families according to the social and emotional climate existing for marriage, i.e. to attempt to establish what is actually happening in society so as to be properly informed about current and future needs.

(ii) To examine the implications of observable contradictions in social values which inform choices and are likely to influence the development of marriage as a social institution and as a base for child rearing.

(iii) To investigate patterns of environmental support which are conducive to individual growth and development within marriage—i.e. investigations which recognize the crucial nature and the complexity of the interplay of the 'inner' with the 'outer' world for individuals and their relationships, and are therefore adequate to inform those concerned with the development of preventive measures.

(b) *Clinical studies* stemming from therapeutic practice in the field, especially that of 'advanced centres'. These should aim :

(i) To improve diagnostic skills and to establish prognostic criteria —i.e. in relation to identifiable categories, to ask the question : Why did these marriages/families encounter difficulty? Why at this particular time? Why in this particular way?

(ii) To develop techniques of work appropriate to different kinds and qualities of marital interaction.

(iii) To identify the settings/agencies most appropriate to different 'clinical' types of marriage and different ways of exposing difficulty together with the factors which route them to these.

(iv) To assess the outcome of therapeutic and preventive intervention and to establish criteria for this.

(c) *Training studies* involving professional educators and agencies in the field, especially those concerned with interdisciplinary training (1, 6, 20, 23).

(i) To develop and evaluate a range of training methods for marital work and the optimum points in professional development for its introduction and extension.

(ii) To consider the in-service training procedures appropriate to different settings and services.

(iii) To examine training programmes and consultation procedures in relation to field problems—i.e. to subject these to the question : Are they making maximum use of the limited resources of skilled manpower?

(d) *Organizational studies* drawing upon the experience of workers concerned with organizational stress, change and adaptation, and of operational research (12, 16, 19).

(i) To investigate problems of inter-agency collaboration in this field.

(ii) To examine the structure and organization of specialist service agencies in relation to their primary task, namely, the treatment of marital problems—i.e. the ways in which, and whether, these help or hinder casework/clinical practice and professional development.

(iii) To consider the organizational strategies required to meet emergent needs. Some would be revealed by studies under (c) above, others, e.g. the needs of those who divorce and their families, have already been exposed.

A coherent programme of research cannot but be ambitious, technically difficult and beyond the competence of existing agencies. But though additional resources and even the development of new institutions are required, all could make valuable contributions if research and development are accepted as indispensable to the functioning of a service agency, and if the right kind of research is undertaken (20, 24).

The most fruitful research is usually that which results from the drive and enthusiasm of inspired and innovative individuals rather than from work undertaken 'on demand'. Nevertheless, there is a pressing need for a map of the field, the details of which would be filled out progressively by specific projects. Such a map is also necessary to establish links between this work and that in related fields. I have in mind, for example, that concerned with the outcome of psychotherapy, with studies in community mental health, with those in the field of social change and social value (10, 12, 19).

The problems listed above are among those which suggest themselves for urgent investigation in the light of experience. They have still to be defined in operational terms; others may well propose additional or alternative work, no doubt with a different emphasis. But plans for a total community service for marriage and marital problems will be ill conceived unless, parallel with them, there is a major investment in collaborative research related to social action. Effective service and the training so extensively required for the future are dependent upon the outcome of such studies.

It is salutary to reflect that though there have been positive developments in community services in the intervening years, the same plea for the basic research necessary to underpin an effective 'marriage welfare service' was made to the Denning Committee (26) in 1947 (21). There can be no doubt that at this stage in the development of community provision, failure to make a planned investment in research in all the areas mentioned above, will be felt even more acutely during the next twenty years than it has been in the past two decades (19).

LIST OF WORKS REFERRED TO IN CHAPTER 9

1. Balint, E. (1959). 'Training post-graduate students in social casework.' *Brit. J. Med. Psychol.*, 32, pp. 193-9
2. Bannister, K., et al. (1955). *Social casework in marital problems: the development of a psychodynamic approach.* London, Tavistock Publications.
3. Bannister, K., and Pincus, L. (1965). *Shared phantasy in marital problems: therapy in a four-person relationship.* Hitchin, The Codicote Press.
4. Bott, R. (1957). *Family and social network: roles, norms and external relationships in ordinary urban families.* London, Social Science Paperbacks, 1968.
5. Dicks, H. V. (1967). *Marital Tensions.* London, Routledge and Kegan Paul.
6. Family Discussion Bureau (1962). *The marital relationship as a focus for casework.* Hitchin, The Codicote Press.
7. Family Discussion Bureau (1966). 'Evidence to the Lord Chancellor's Committee on the age of majority.' Document T 791 (unpublished).
8. Family Discussion Bureau and Marital Unit, Tavistock Clinic (1966). 'Some implications of marital stress for a comprehensive social service for the family. Evidence to the Committee on Local Authority and Allied Personal Social Services.' Document F.D.B. 20 (unpublished).
9. Family Discussion Bureau (1968). 'Memorandum on the Divorce Reform Bill.' Document F.D.B. 32 (unpublished).
10. Malan, D. H. (1963). *A study of brief psychotherapy* (Mind

and Medicine Monograph, no. 8). London, Tavistock Publications.
11. Menzies, I. E. P. (1960). 'A case-study in the functioning of social systems as a defence against anxiety : a report on a study of the nursing service of a general hospital.' *Human Relations*, 13, pp. 95-121.
12. Miller, E. J., and Rice, A. K. (1967). *Systems of organization. The control of task and sentient boundaries.* London, Tavistock Publications.
13. Philp, A. F. (1963). *Family failure.* London, Faber and Faber.
14. Pincus, L. ed. (1960). *Marriage: studies in emotional conflict and growth.* London, Methuen.
15. Rapoport, R., and Rapoport, R. N. (1969). 'The dual career family.' *Human Relations*, 22, pp. 3-29.
16. Rice, A. K. (1965). *Learning for leadership. Interpersonal and intergroup relations.* London, Tavistock Publications.
17. Sutherland, J. D. (1956). 'Psychotherapy and social casework', in Goldberg, E. M., ed., *The boundaries of casework.* London, Assn. of Psych. Soc. Wkrs, pp. 22-35.
18. Sutherland, J. D. (1967). 'The place of psychotherapy in community mental health' (The Margaret Allan Lecture). Edinburgh, *Contact*, 19, pp. 2-18.
19. Trist, E. (1968). *The relation of welfare and development in the transition to post-industrialism.* Socio-technical Systems Division, Western Management Science Institute, University of California, Los Angeles.
20. Wilson, A. T. M. (1947). 'The development of a scientific basis in family casework', *Social Work*, 4, 62-9.
21. Wilson, A. T. M. (1949). 'Some reflections and suggestions on the prevention and treatment of marital problems.' *Human Relations*, 2, pp. 233-51.
22. Woodhouse, D. L. (1961). 'Psychiatric influences in community services, II', in Irvine, E. E. ed., *Ventures in professional co-operation,* London, Assn. of Psych. Soc. Wkrs, pp. 64-76.
23. Woodhouse, D. L. (1964). 'Short residential courses for post-graduate social workers', in Gosling, R., *et al., The use of small groups in training.* Hitchin, The Codicote Press in conjunction with the Tavistock Institute of Medical Psychology, pp. 76-97.
24. — 'Principles of research.' Tavistock Institute of Human Relations, Document A 913 (unpublished).
25. — (1966). *Putting asunder: a divorce law for contemporary society.* London, S.P.C.K.
26. — (1947). *Committee on procedure in Matrimonial Causes,* Cmd. 7024. London, H.M.S.O.

Notes on the Contributors

Quentin de la Bedoyere has for a number of years been working with engaged couples and is a member of the Wimbledon Centre of the Catholic Marriage Advisory Council.

Jack Dominian is a consultant psychiatrist who has also been a medical adviser to the Catholic Marriage Advisory Council since 1958, where he conducts case-discussions with marriage counsellors. He is the author of the Pelican Original *Marital Breakdown* (1968); and of *Psychiatry and the Christian* (1962) and *Christian Marriage* (1967).

Gordon R. Dunstan is F.D. Maurice Professor of Moral and Social Theology at King's College, London, Canon Theologian of Leicester Cathedral and a priest-in-ordinary to Her Majesty the Queen. As former Secretary to the Church Assembly Board for Social Responsibility he has been closely associated with the development of the Anglican theology of sex and marriage. He is editor of the journal *Theology*.

Rosemary Haughton is a wife, mother, author and broadcaster on both television and radio. Her writings have given many a new insight into the Bible, theology, and the meaning of human relationships.

John Marshall is a neurologist and is a member of the Catholic Marriage Advisory Council Executive Committee and of its General Medical Committee. He was a member of the papal commission on birth-control. He has written a number of books including *Preparing for Marriage*.

Patricia Marshall is a wife, mother, general practitioner and former secretary of the Newcastle Centre of the Catholic Marriage Advisory Council. She is a member of the CMAC Executive Committee, and editor of its quarterly Bulletin. She also broadcasts and has appeared on television in discussions of marital and family problems.

Denis F. O'Callaghan is Professor of Moral Theology at St Patrick's College, Maynooth, where he gives the theological course on marriage. He has contributed many articles to the professional journals on this theme.

Bernard Parker is a consultant gynaecologist and Chairman of the Medical Advisory Committee of the Catholic Marriage Advisory Council.

Douglas Woodhouse is a psychiatric social worker who is Chairman of the Staff Executive Committee of the Institute of Marital Studies. This Institute, which was formerly known as the Family Discussion Bureau, has been engaged in the study of marital problems in depth for a number of years past.

MARRIAGE ANNULMENT

A Practical guide for Roman Catholics and others
Ralph Brown

There is a serious need for a comprehensive guide to Roman Catholic law and procedure to help couples who are unhappy or unsuccessfully married. Ralph Brown is an officer in the Archdiocese of Westminster's annulment courts and has had much experience in this field. He is therefore well-equipped to provide a practical guide to the questions that arise.

What makes a marriage legal in the eyes of the Church? What procedures have to be followed to take an annulment case through the Church courts? On what grounds can a marriage be declared null and void? Clear, simple and complete answers to these questions can be found here.

All grounds for nullity and invalidity are fully explained and examples of case histories are given. In addition, the reader will find a step-by-step description of the workings of the Church's annulment courts.

Over fifty per cent of all persons who are dealt with by the Roman Catholic Church's marriage courts are, in fact, not themselves Catholics. *Marriage Annulment* will therefore be of importance to members of all denominations who are contemplating the annulment of marriage, and to whom the Catholic Church's view of the validity of marriage is a very real problem.

ISBN 0 225.48895.7   23s (£1.15p)